AF572454

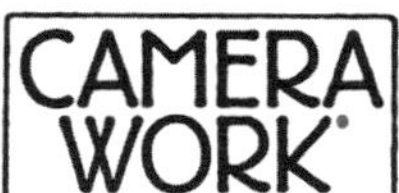

Time and Silence

Caroline Halley des Fontaines

teNeues

Voyage from the heavens to the earth,
voyage from the eternal toward the ephemeral,
voyage through knowledge,
meeting the people of the world.

Reise vom Himmel zur Erde,
Reise vom Ewigen zum Vergänglichen,
Reise zum Wissen,
den Menschen der Erde begegnend.

Voyage du ciel vers la terre,
voyage de l'éternel vers l'éphémère,
voyage à travers les connaissances,
rencontres avec les peuples de la Terre.

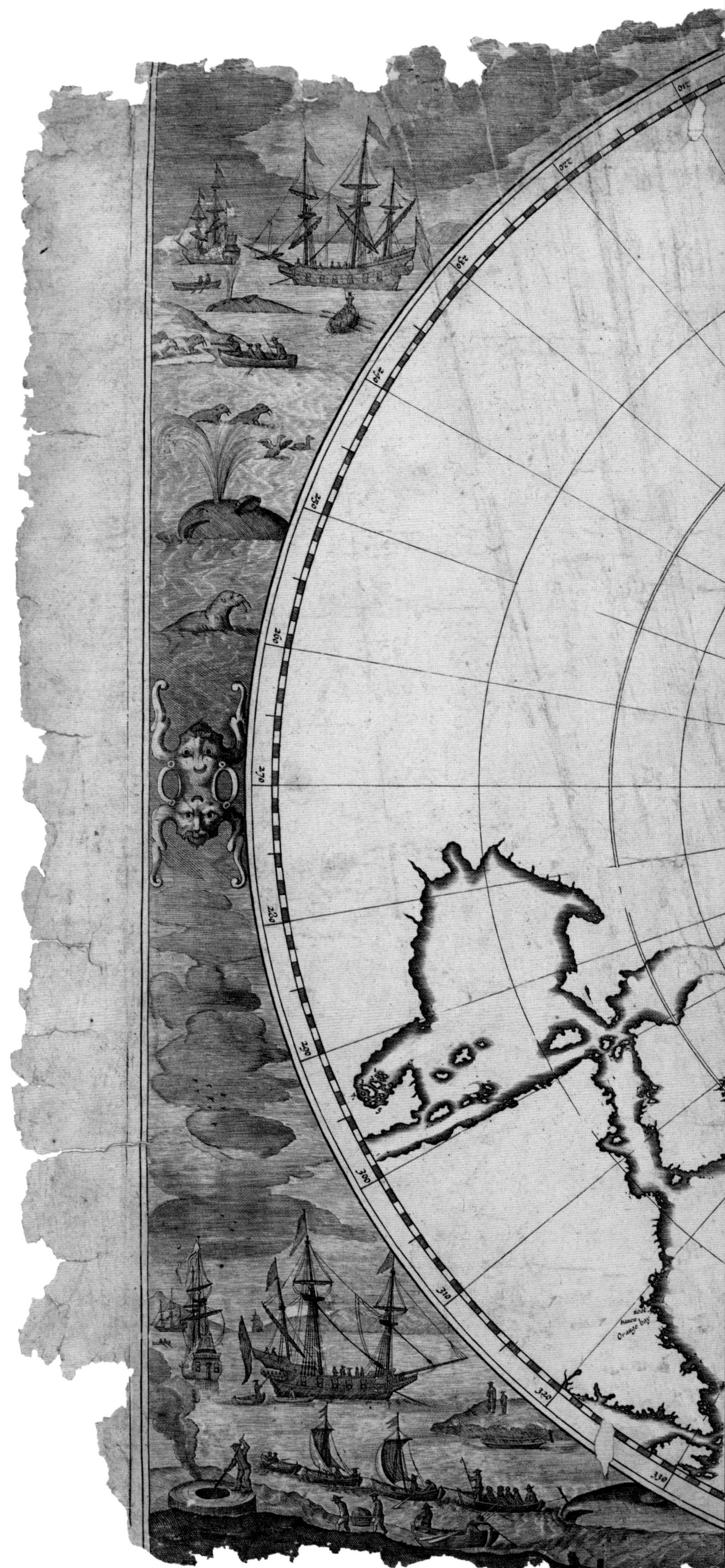

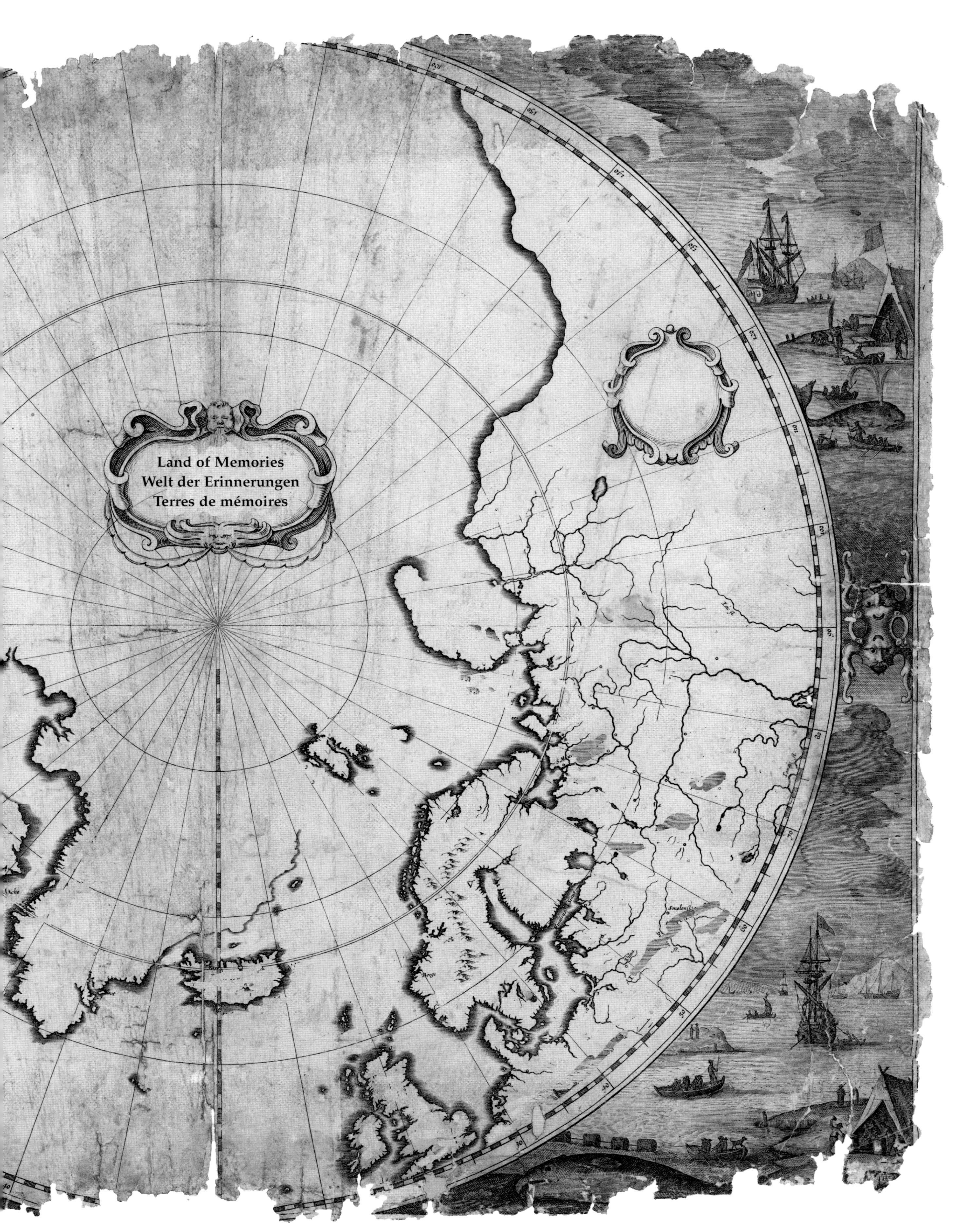

Land of Memories
Welt der Erinnerungen
Terres de mémoires

Time and Silence

I followed your whispers across oceans and deserts.
In between times and silences,
I looked for you in unknown landscapes
that seemed only possible in the sacred imagination of painters.
I saw women threshing wheat on doorsteps,
and the old ones waiting for the passing of clouds.
Children lit fires all along the paths,
and scattered them with flowers that pierced the sky like stars.
Songs came and went from the center of the earth,
Accompanied by silence.
Silence became song.
Days and nights went by.
I left for the white desert, there,
The temples of men rose against the skies.
Time turned the stones to the color of eternity.
In the distance, a child, the sand, a pyramid became one.
The perfume of incense lingered in smokes that led to invisible gardens.
I walked with a man they call the Guardian of Isis to the top of a mountain
and together we lit candles illuminating the valley lost in fog.
Women and children prayed for salvation calling upon the black sun.
An old woman spoke of all she had seen—
thousands of white birds descending from the sky,
carrying away the children who longed to see the ocean,
then they were transformed into rivers
that cross the world to extinguish the fires of men.
The children never returned
but the rivers colored the flowers and the landscapes.
Since then days come and go
and I walk along the river banks
with the echo of your whispers as my only guide.
Sometimes I stare at the sky,
hoping secretly
to see a white bird born from the clouds,
the ancient Phoenix.

Caroline Halley des Fontaines

Zeit und Stille

Auf deinem Murmeln bin ich durch Wüsten und über Meere gefahren.
Habe dich dort, zwischen Zeit und Stille
In fremden Ländern gesucht,
Die sonst nur die Maler in ihrer göttlichen Imagination erreichen.
Ich sah Frauen auf den Türschwellen Korn dreschen,
Und Alte den Zug der Wolken erwarten.
Am Wegesrand machten die Kinder Feuer,
Und verstreuten dort Blumen, die sich aufreihten wie Himmelssterne.
Aus den Tiefen der Erde kamen Gesänge und gingen,
Ohne die Stille zu verdrängen.
Tage und Nächte vergingen.
Ich bin in die weiße Wüste aufgebrochen,
Dort wo sich die Tempel der Menschen bis zum Himmel erheben.
Die Zeit ist an ihnen vorübergezogen, und der Stein hat die Farbe der Ewigkeit angenommen.
Ein Kind verschmolz mit dem Sand und verwandelte sich in eine Pyramide.
Der Duft von Weihrauchschwaden schien zu unsichtbaren Gärten zu führen.
Oben in den Bergen bin ich bei jenem Mann geblieben, den sie Wächter der Isis nennen,
Und wir haben gemeinsam Kerzen angezündet, die das im Nebel verlorene Tal erhellten.
Frauen und Kinder kamen, um für ihr Heil zu beten, und riefen die schwarze Sonne an.
Eine alte Frau ergriff das Wort.
Sie erzählte, sie habe Tausende weiße Vögel vom Himmel herabstürzen sehen,
Und sie hätten alle Kinder mitgenommen, die das Meer sehen wollten.
Dann verwandelten sie sich in Flüsse,
Die sich über die Welt ausbreiteten, um die Flammen der Menschen zu löschen.
Die Kinder sind nicht zurückgekehrt,
Aber die Flüsse haben den Blumen und Landschaften ihre Farbe wiedergeschenkt.
Seitdem kommen und gehen die Tage,
Und ich wandere mit dem Echo deines Murmelns als einzigem Stern an den Ufern der Flüsse entlang,
Wende manchmal den Blick zum Himmel
Und hoffe im Stillen, dass
Zwischen den Wolken jener weiße Vogel erscheint,
Phoenix aus der Asche.

Caroline Halley des Fontaines

Le temps et le silence

Sur tes murmures, j'ai traversé les mers et les déserts.
Là bas, entre les temps et les silences,
Je t'ai cherché dans des paysages inconnus
Que seuls les peintres auraient pu approcher par le sacré de leur imaginaire.
J'ai vu des femmes battre le blé sur les pas de porte
Et des vieux attendre le passage des nuages.
Les enfants faisaient des feux le long des chemins,
Et y parsemaient des fleurs qui filaient telles les étoiles dans le ciel.
Des chants allaient et venaient du centre de la terre,
Les silences devenaient parallèles.
Des jours et des nuits sont passés.
Je suis partie dans le désert blanc, là bas,
Les temples des hommes s'érigeaient jusqu'aux ciels.
Le temps les avait dépassé et la pierre avait la couleur de l'éternel.
Un enfant se confondait avec le sable, et s'immergeait d'une pyramide.
Les odeurs d'encens persistaient en fumées et semblaient mener à des jardins invisibles.
Je suis restée avec le nommé gardien d'Isis en haut de la montagne,
Et ensemble on a allumé des bougies qui ont éclairé toute la vallée perdue dans le brouillard.
Il y avaient des femmes et des enfants qui venaient prier pour leur salut en invoquant le soleil noir.
Une vieille femme parlait seule,
Elle disait qu'elle avait vu des milliers d'oiseaux blancs descendre du ciel,
Qu'ils avaient emmené tous les enfants qui voulaient voir la mer.
Puis ils se sont transformés en rivières
Qui ont traversé le monde pour éteindre les flammes des hommes.
Les enfants ne sont pas revenus,
Mais les rivières ont redonné la couleur aux fleurs et aux paysages.
Depuis les jours se lèvent et se couchent
Et je marche le long des rives avec comme seule étoile l'écho de tes murmures
Parfois le regard dans le ciel,
En espérant secrètement
Voir naître des nuages cet oiseau blanc,
Phoenix de légende.

Caroline Halley des Fontaines

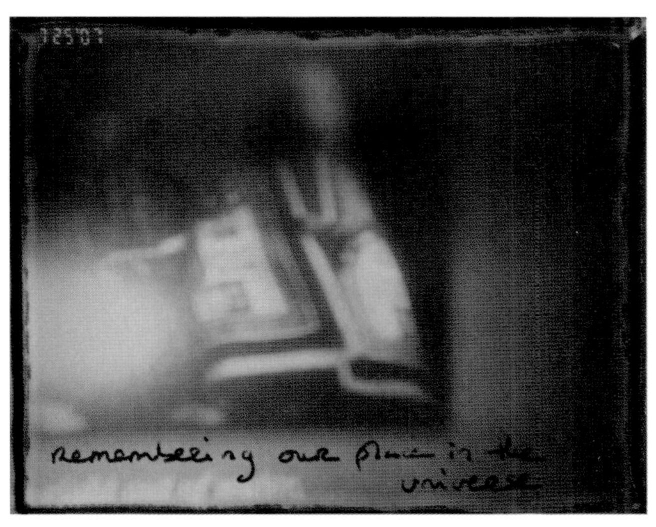
remembering our place in the
universe

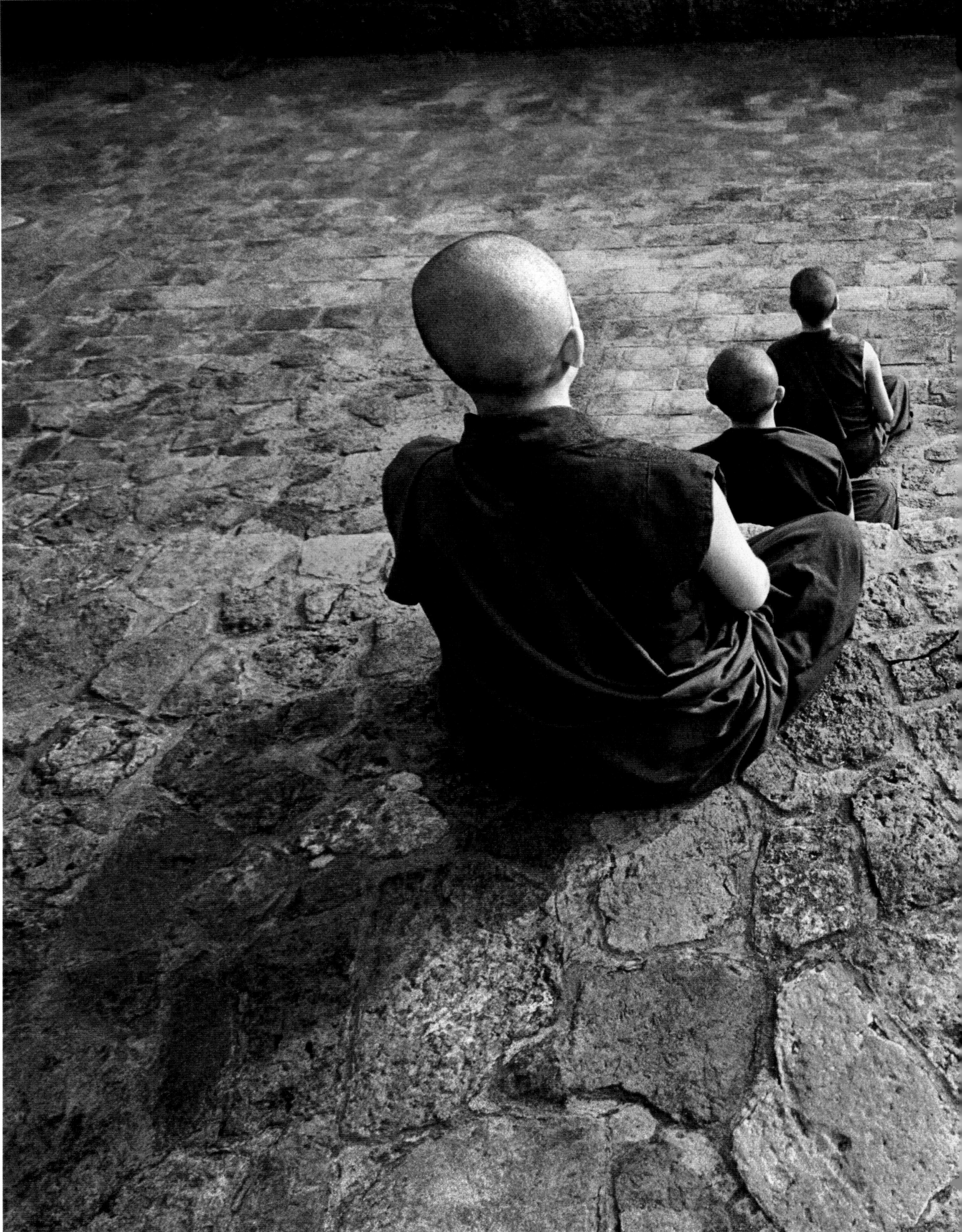

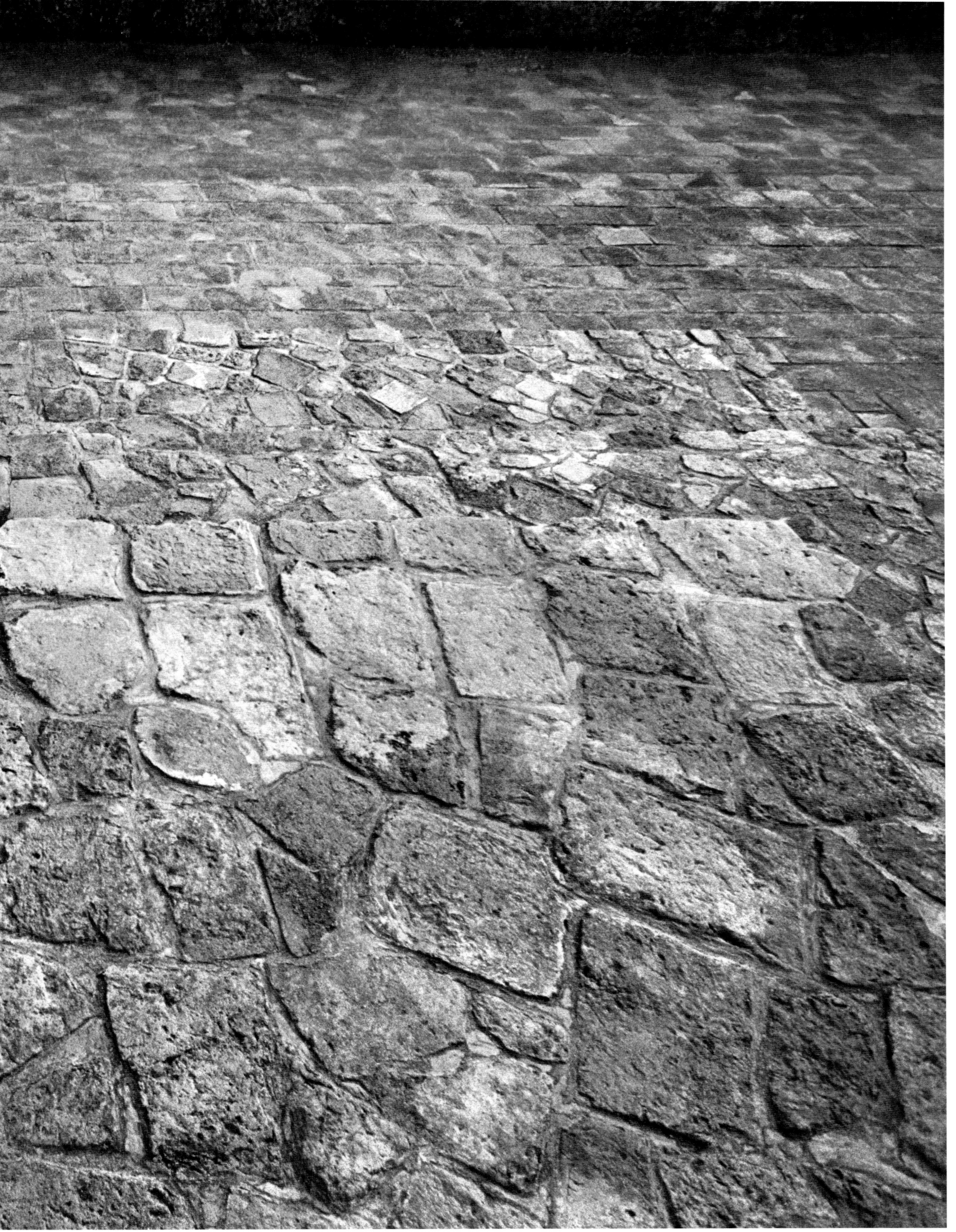

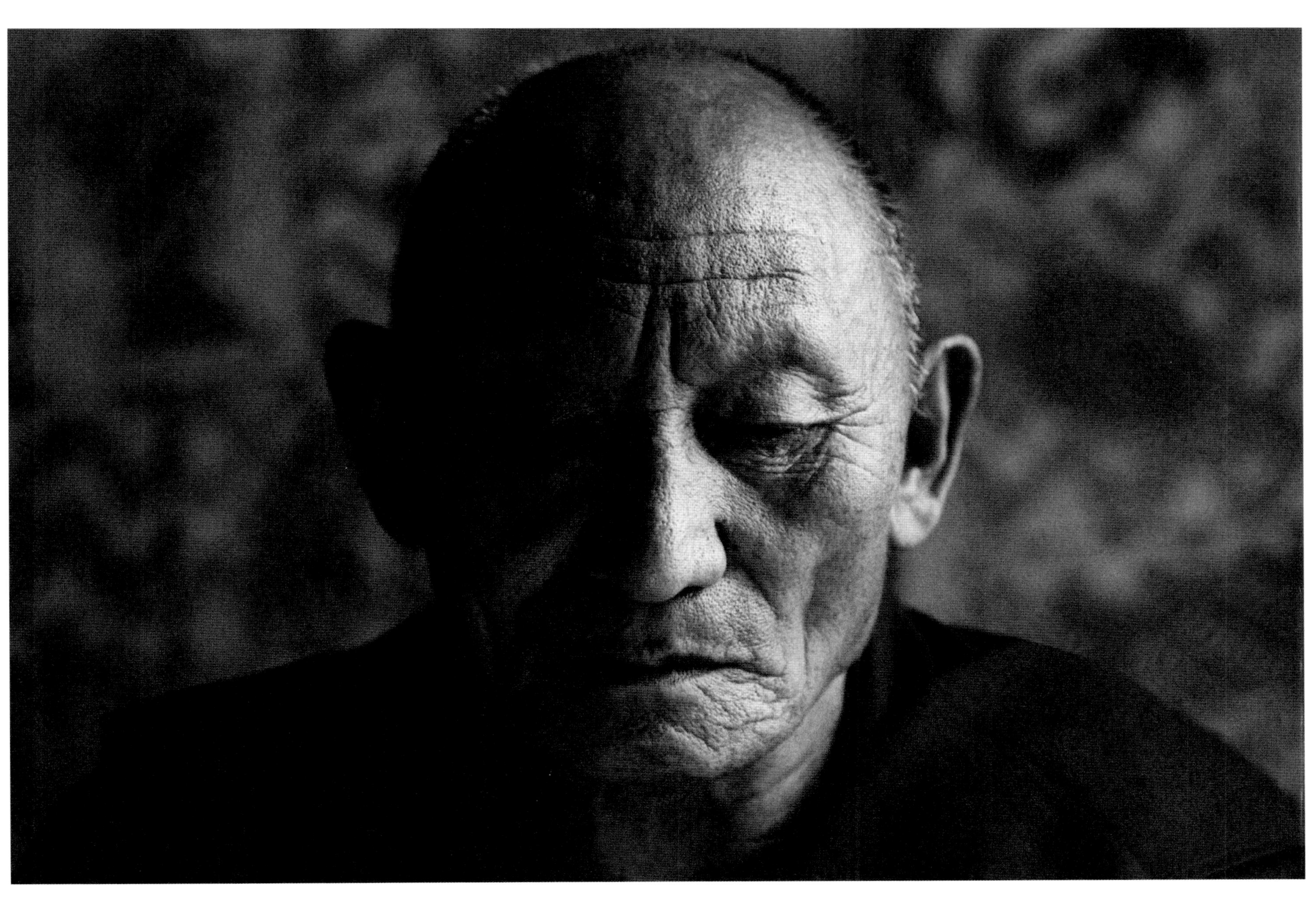

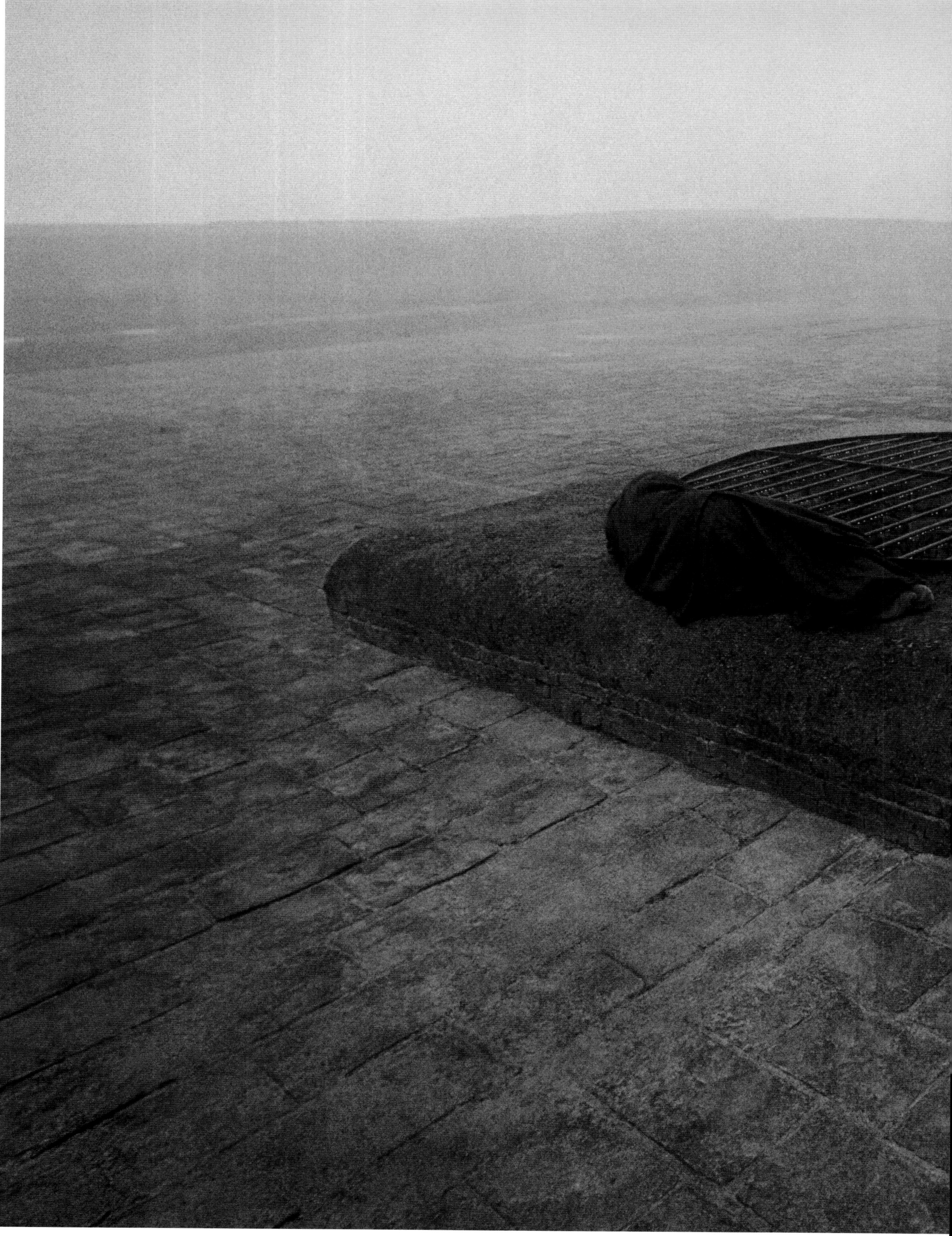

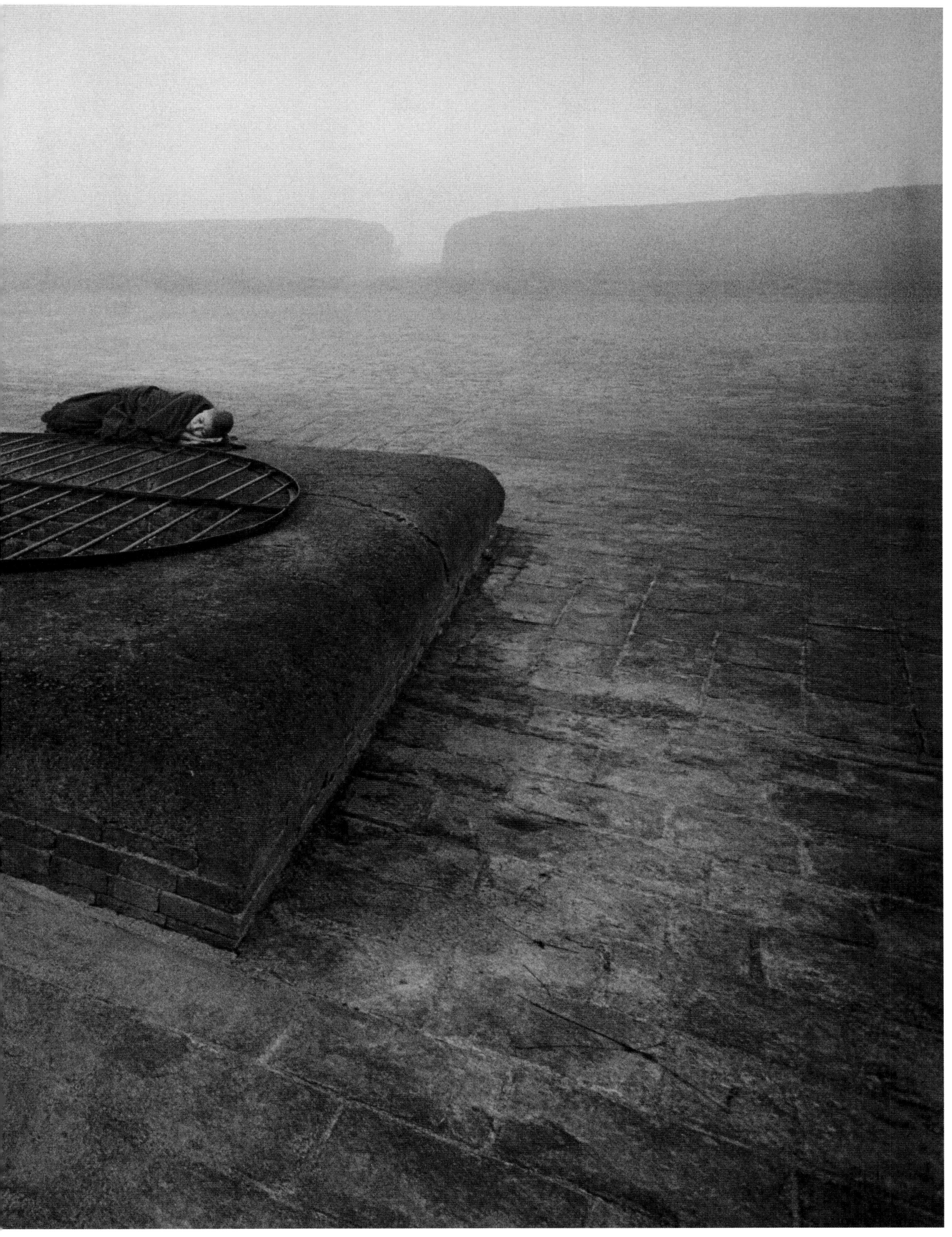

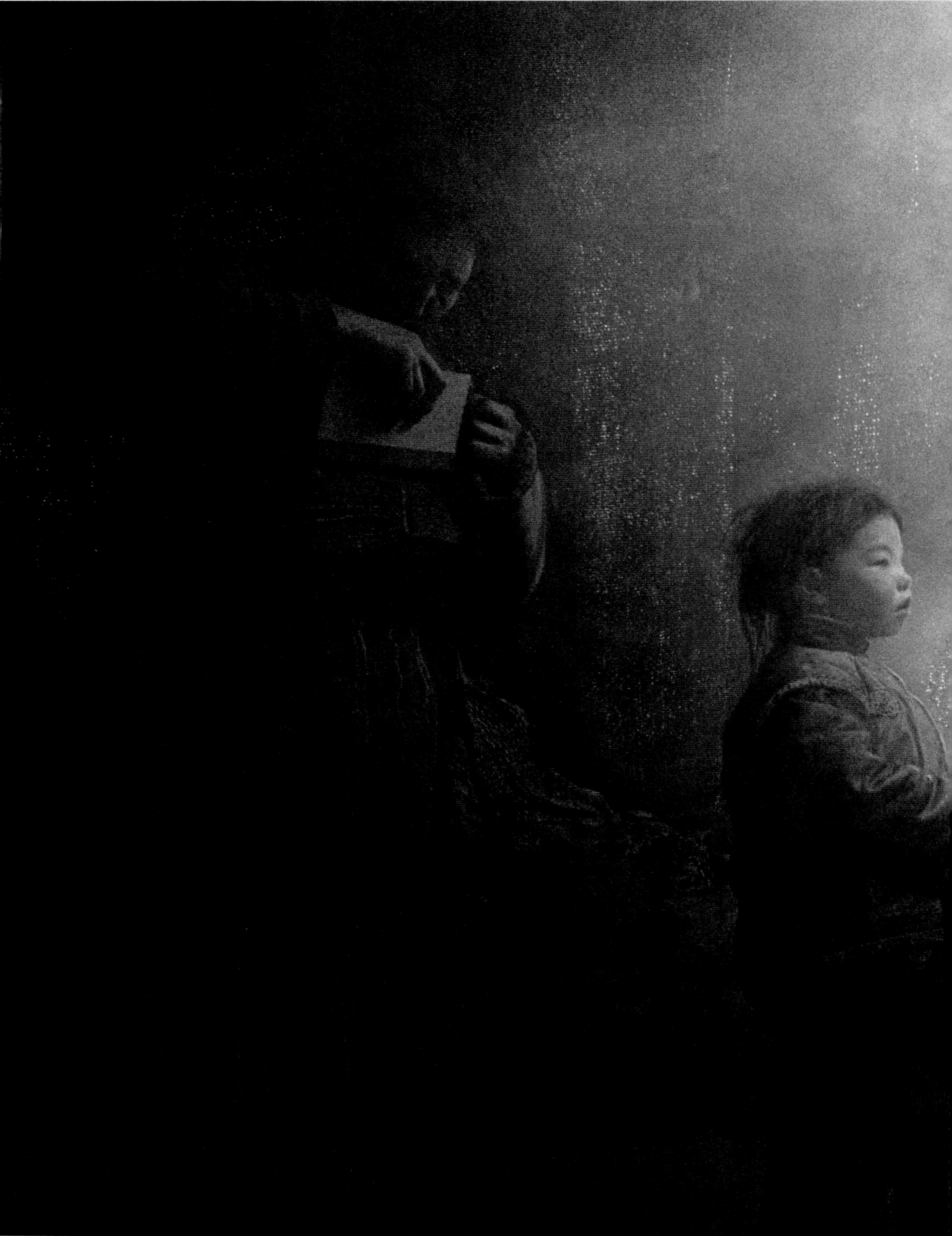

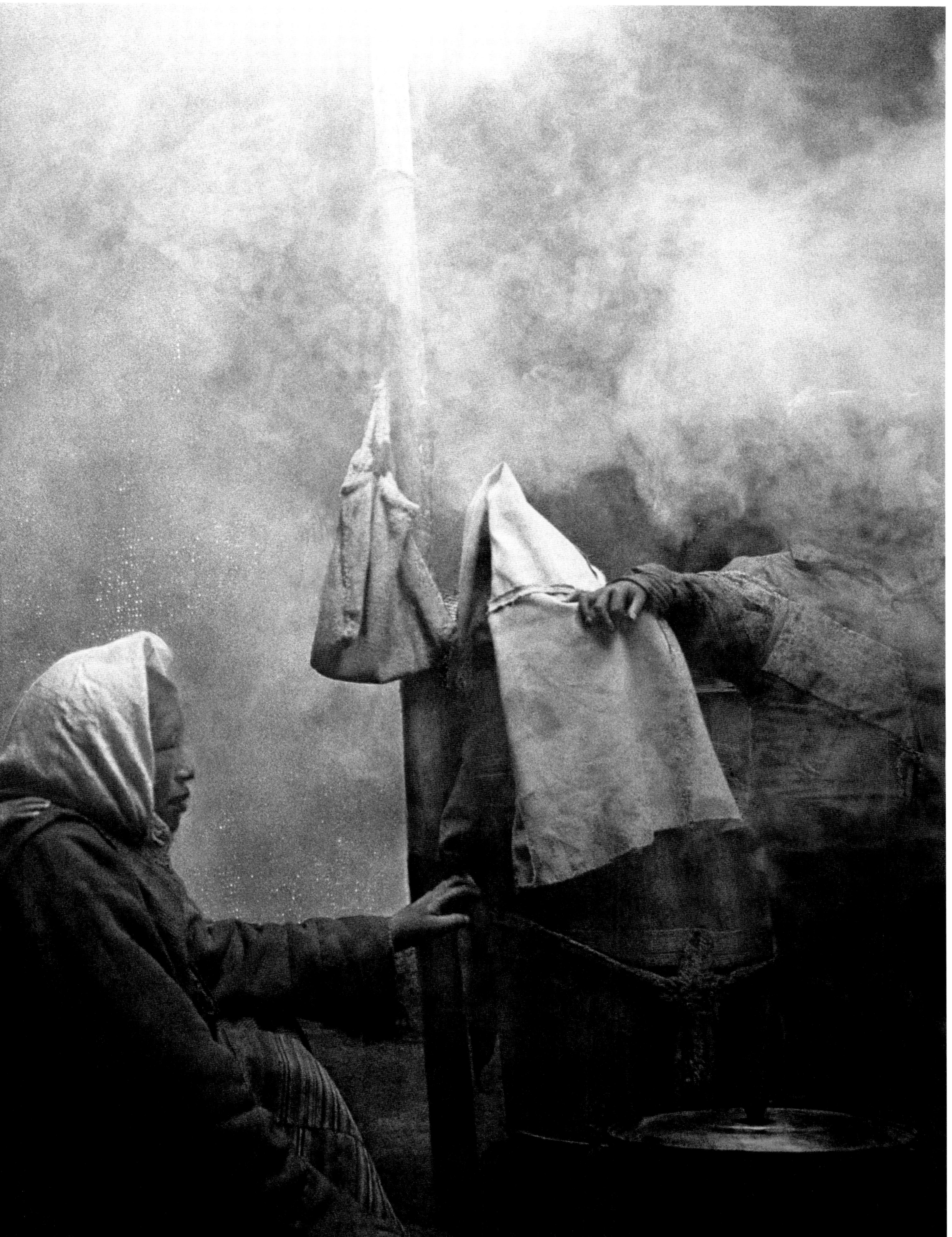

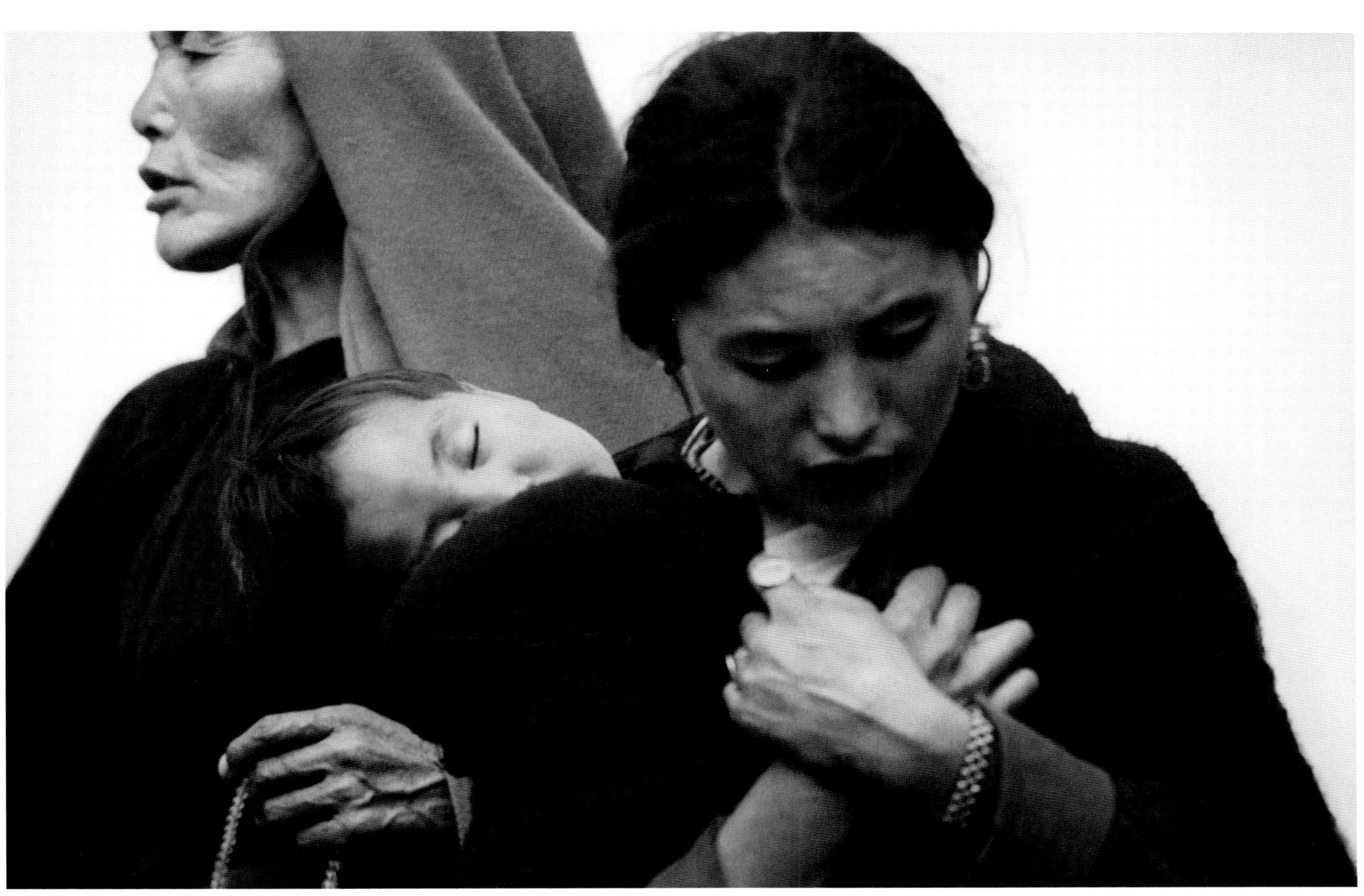

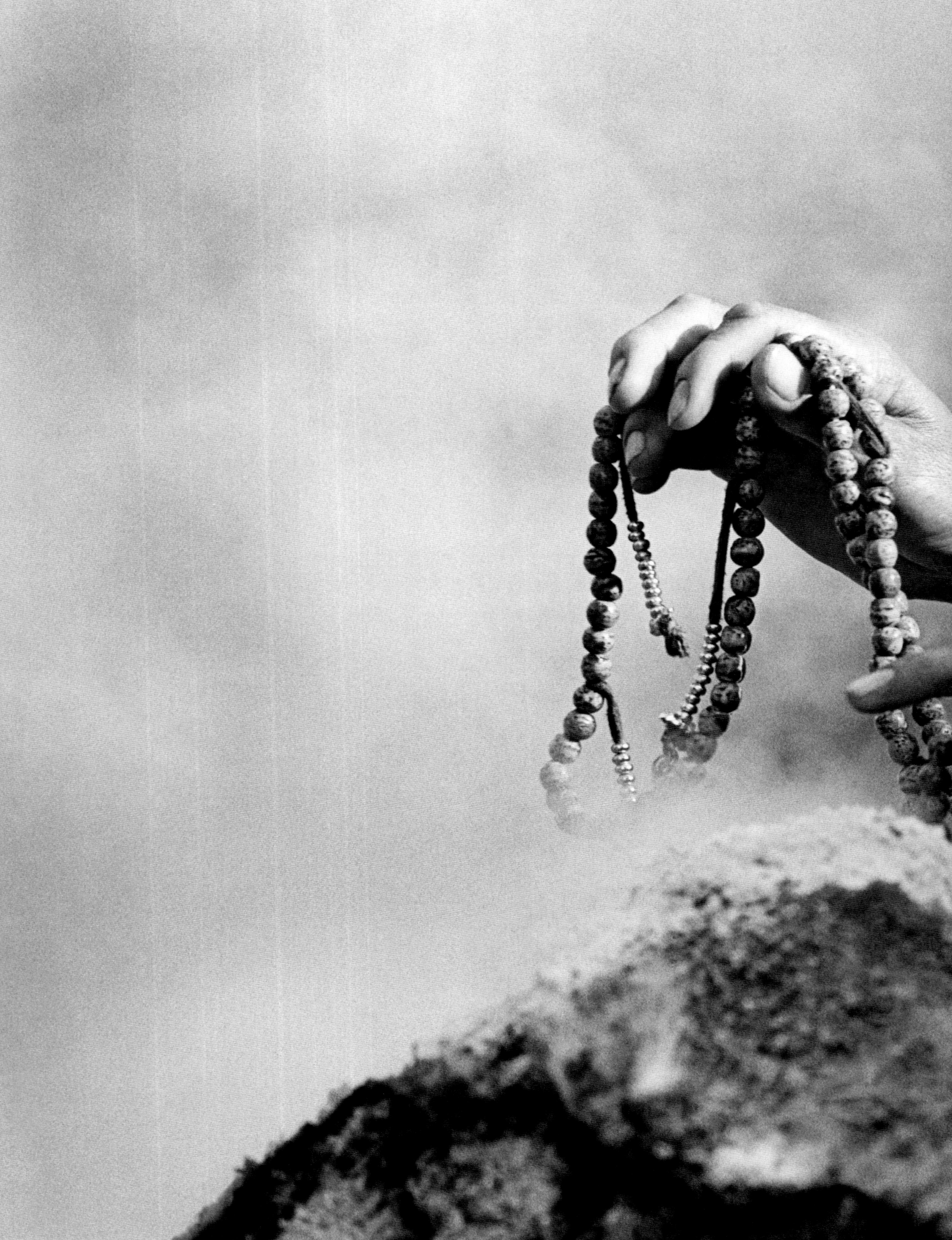

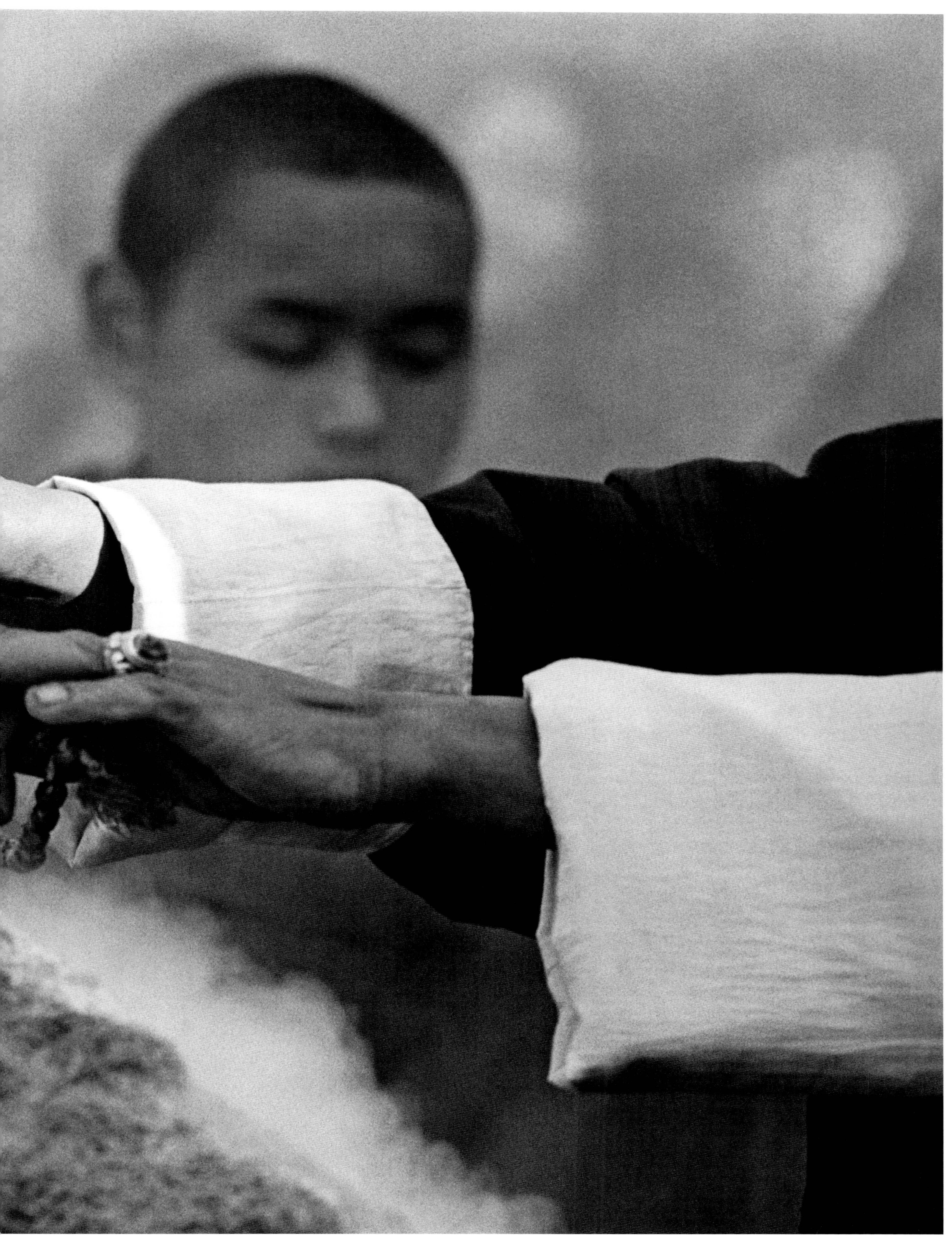

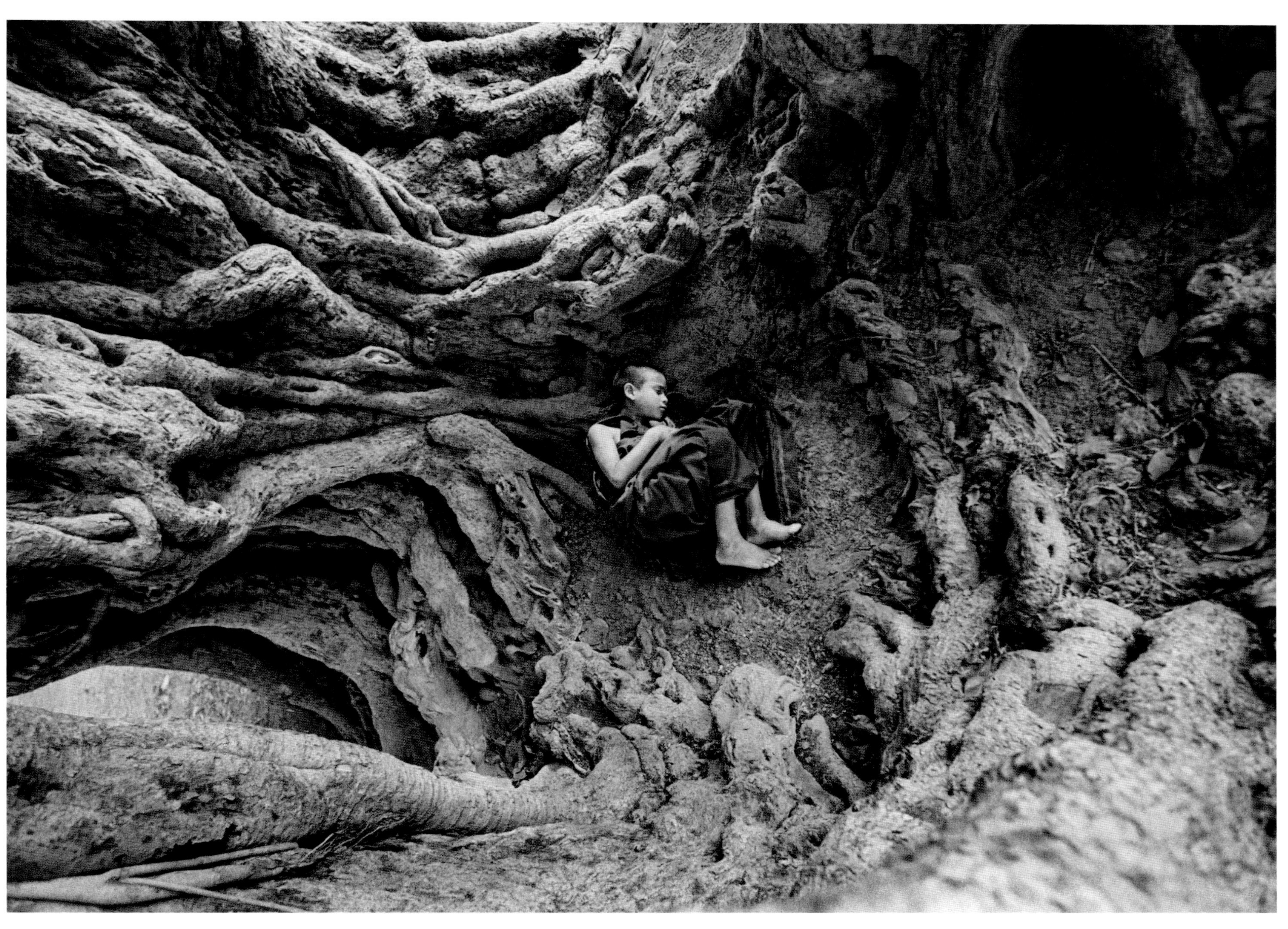

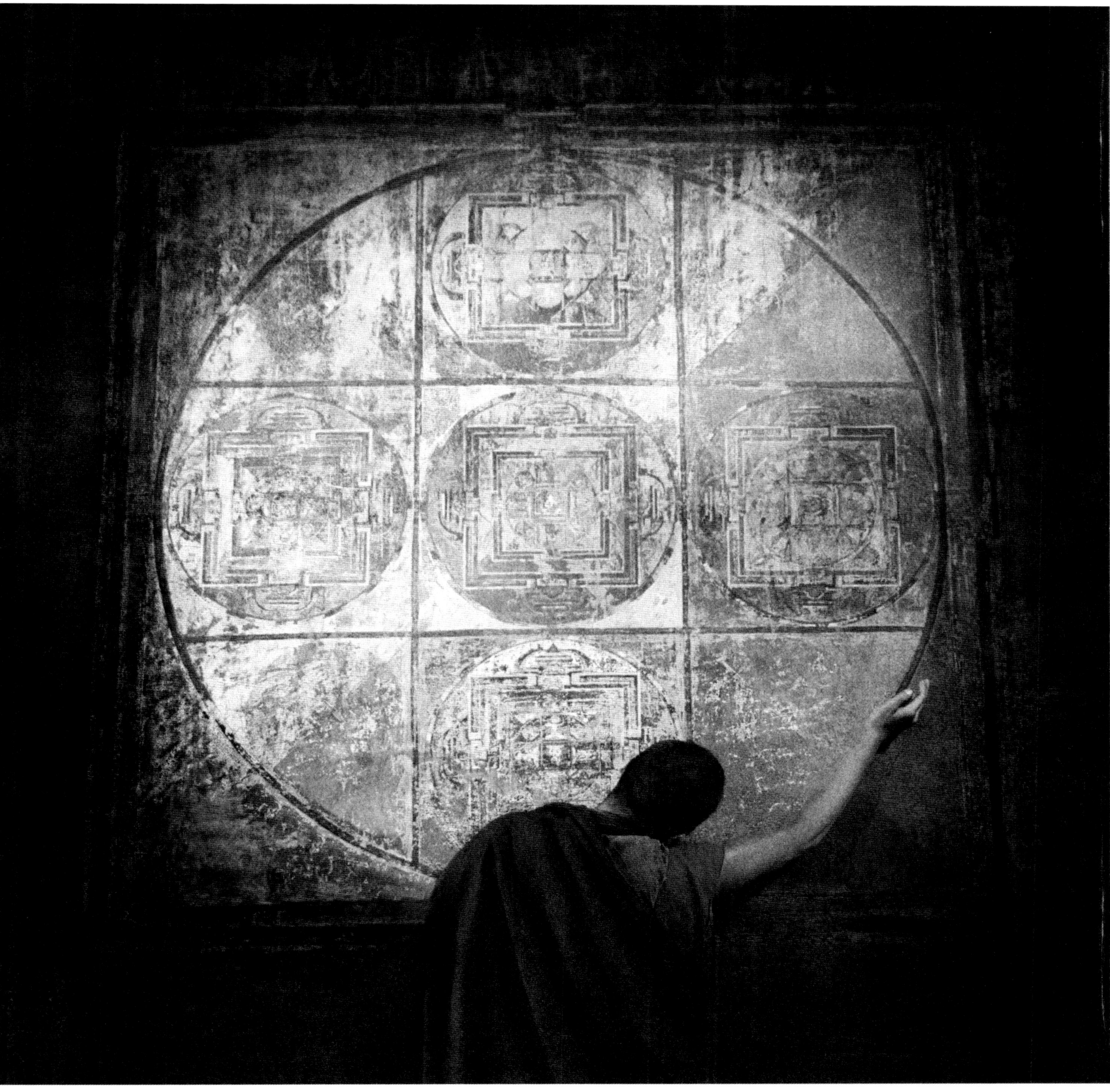

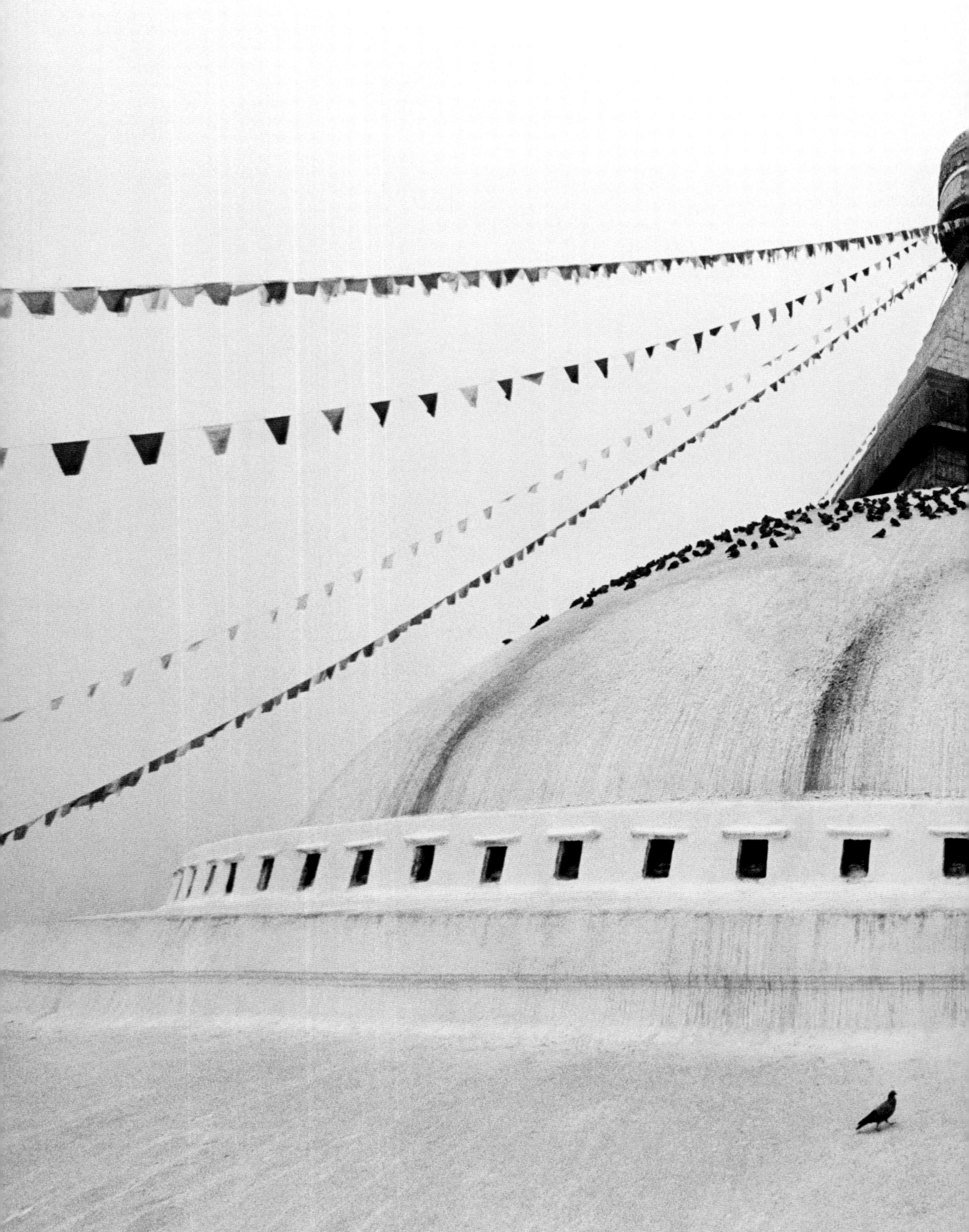

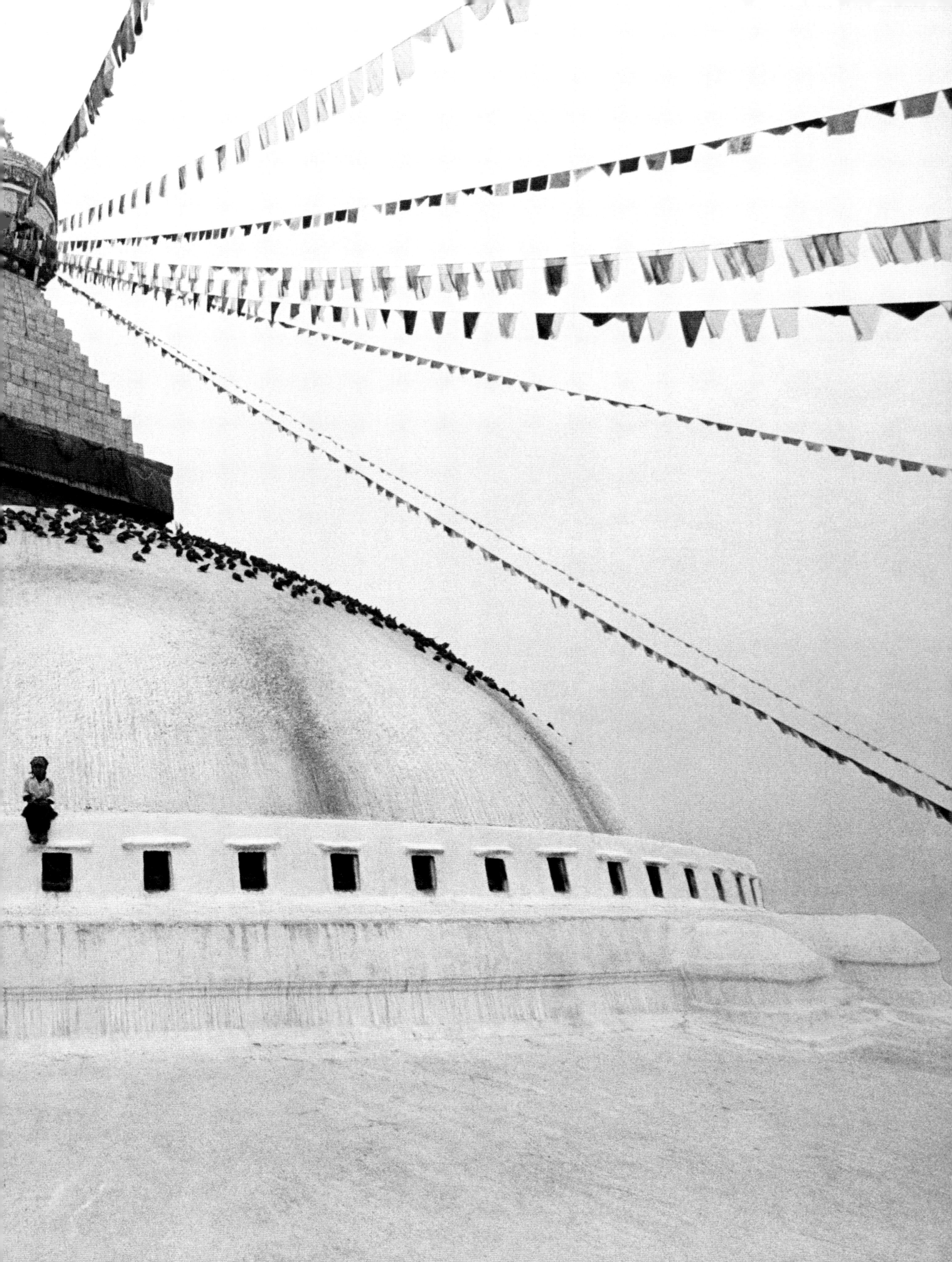

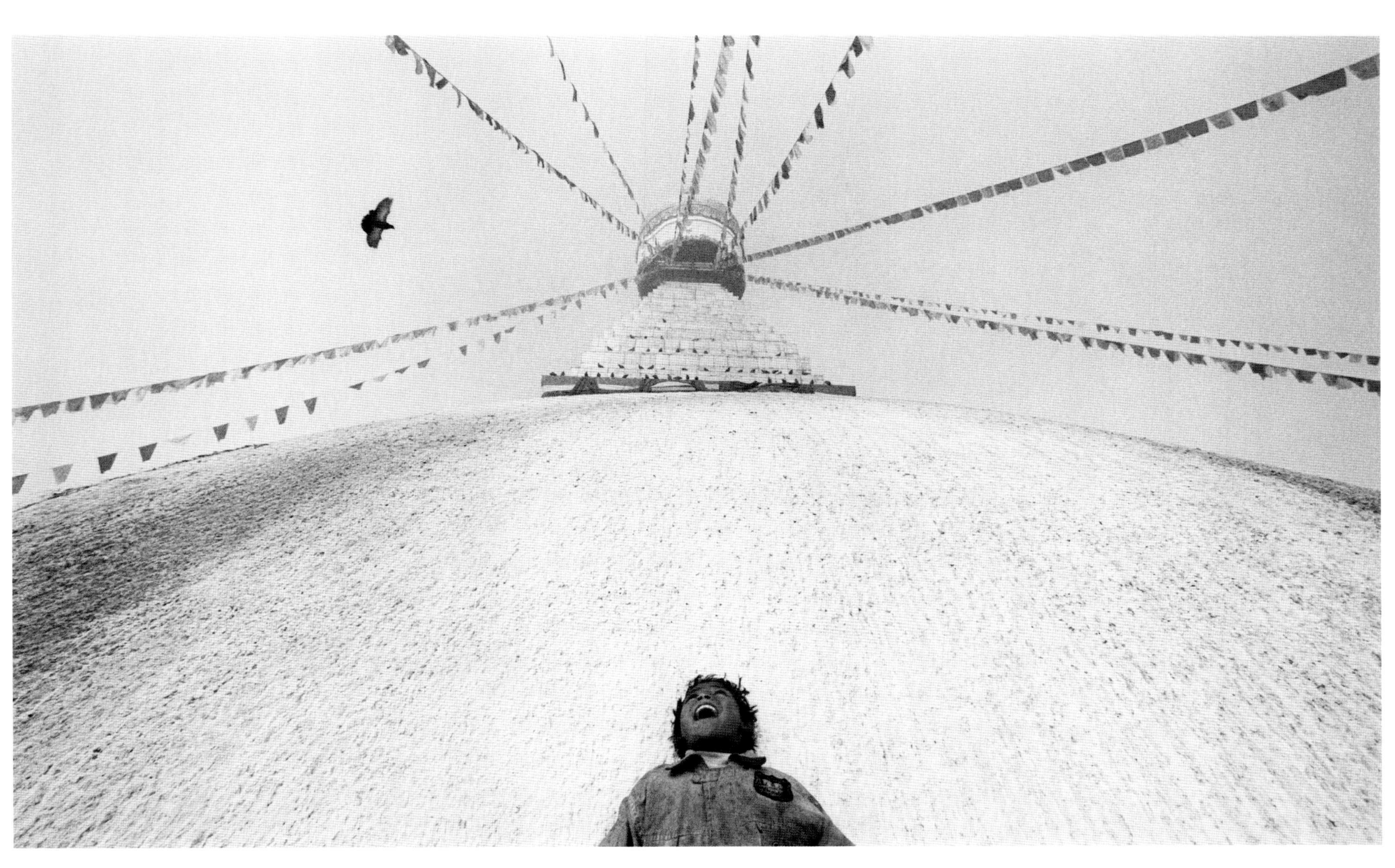

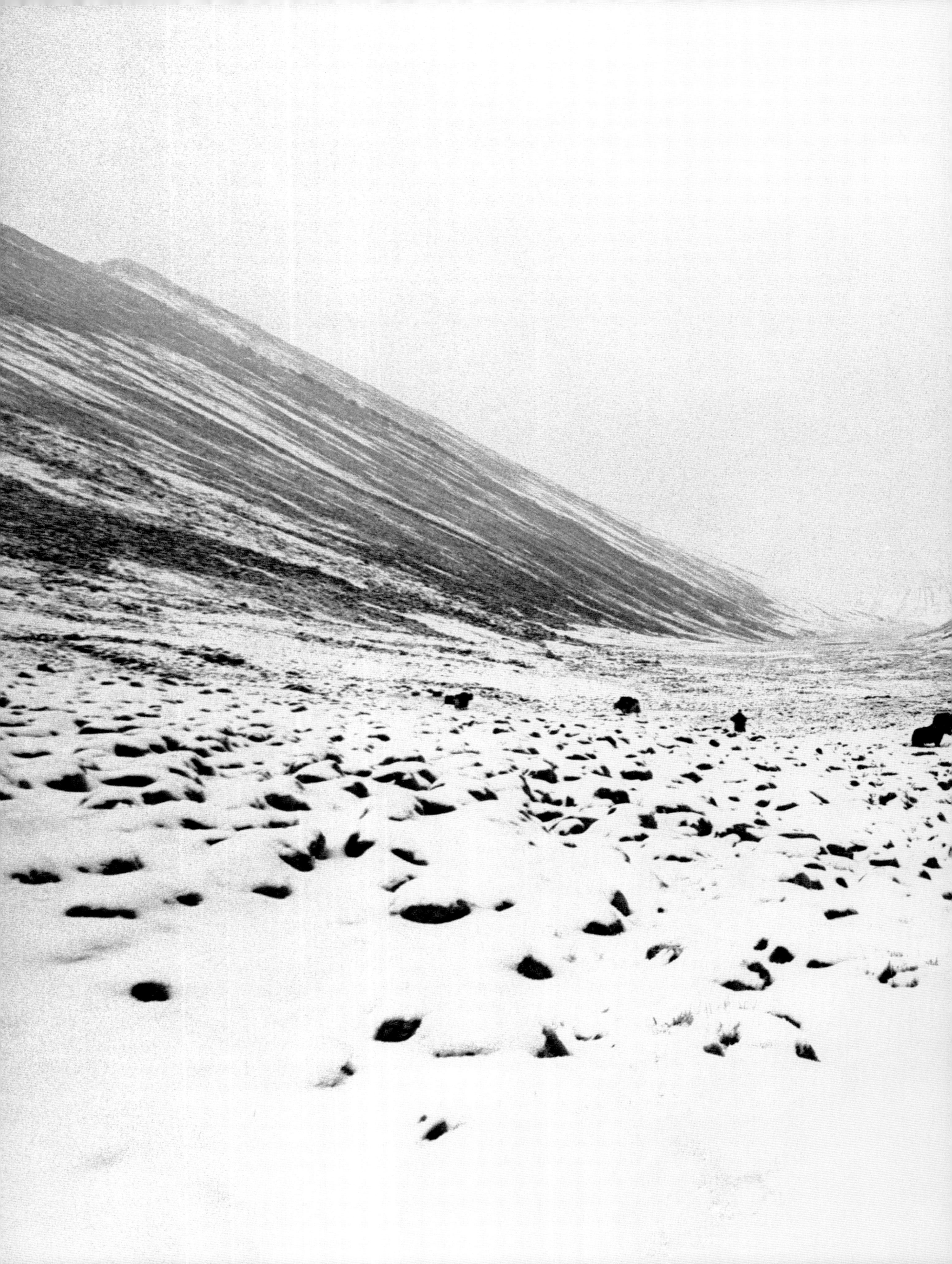

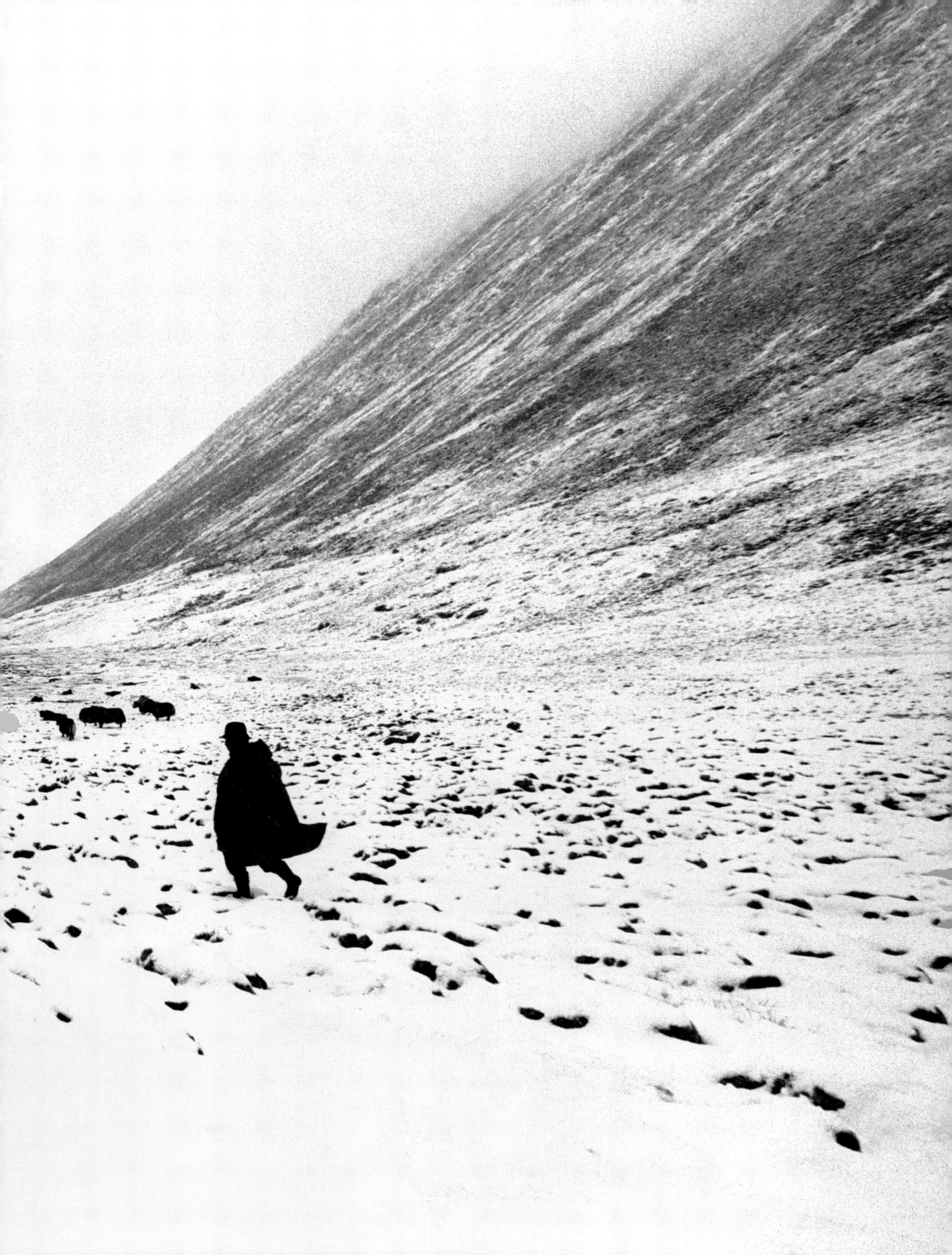

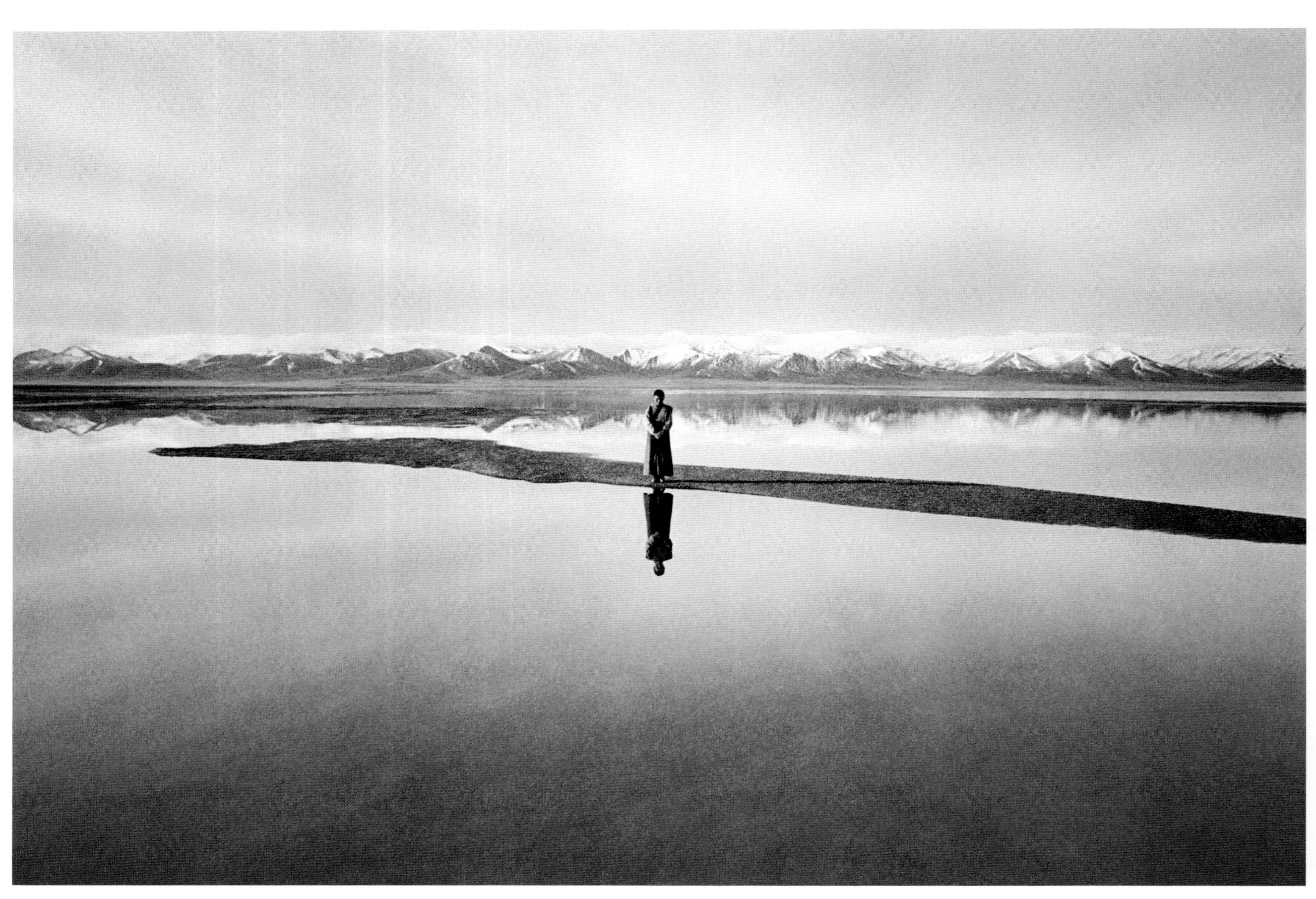

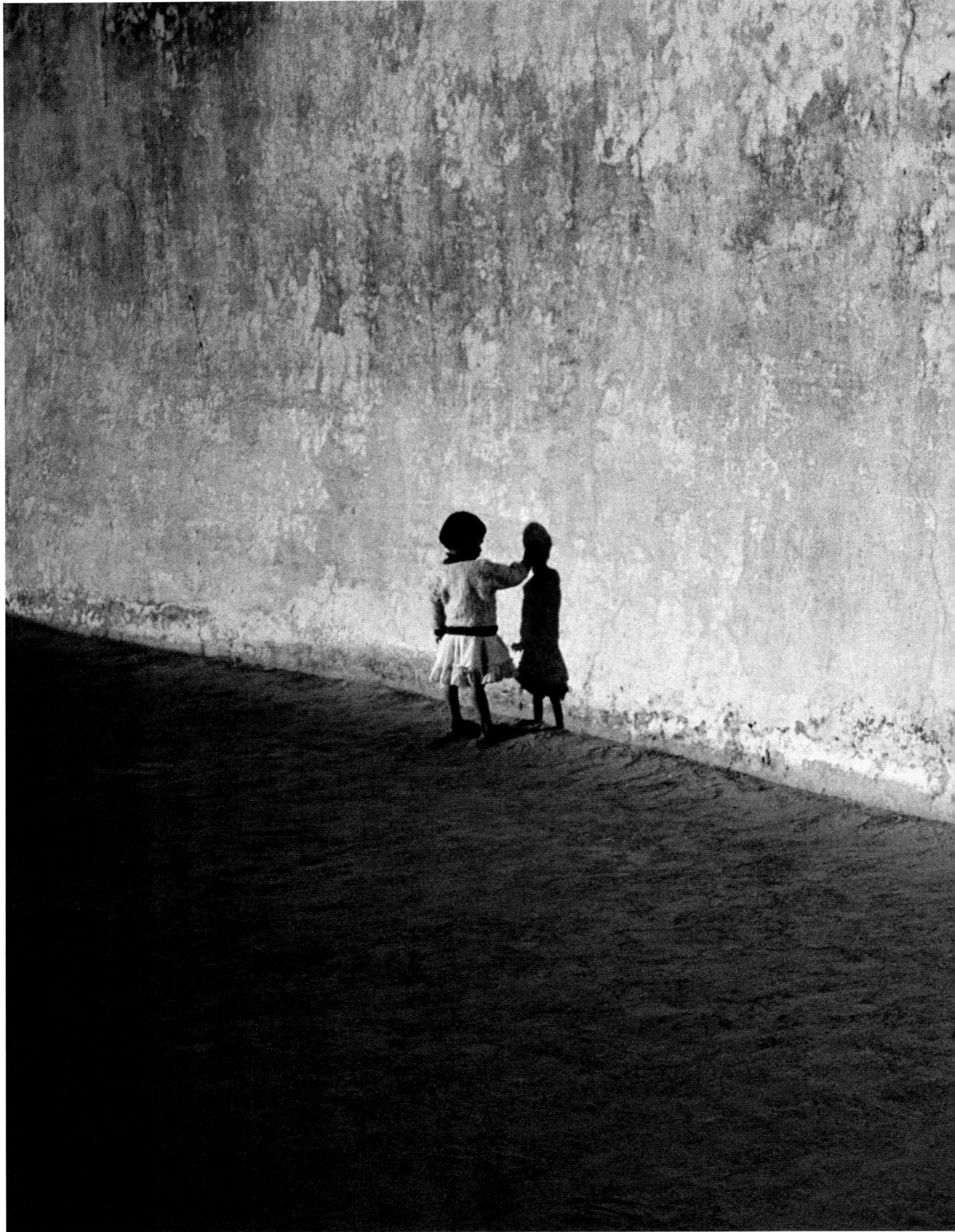

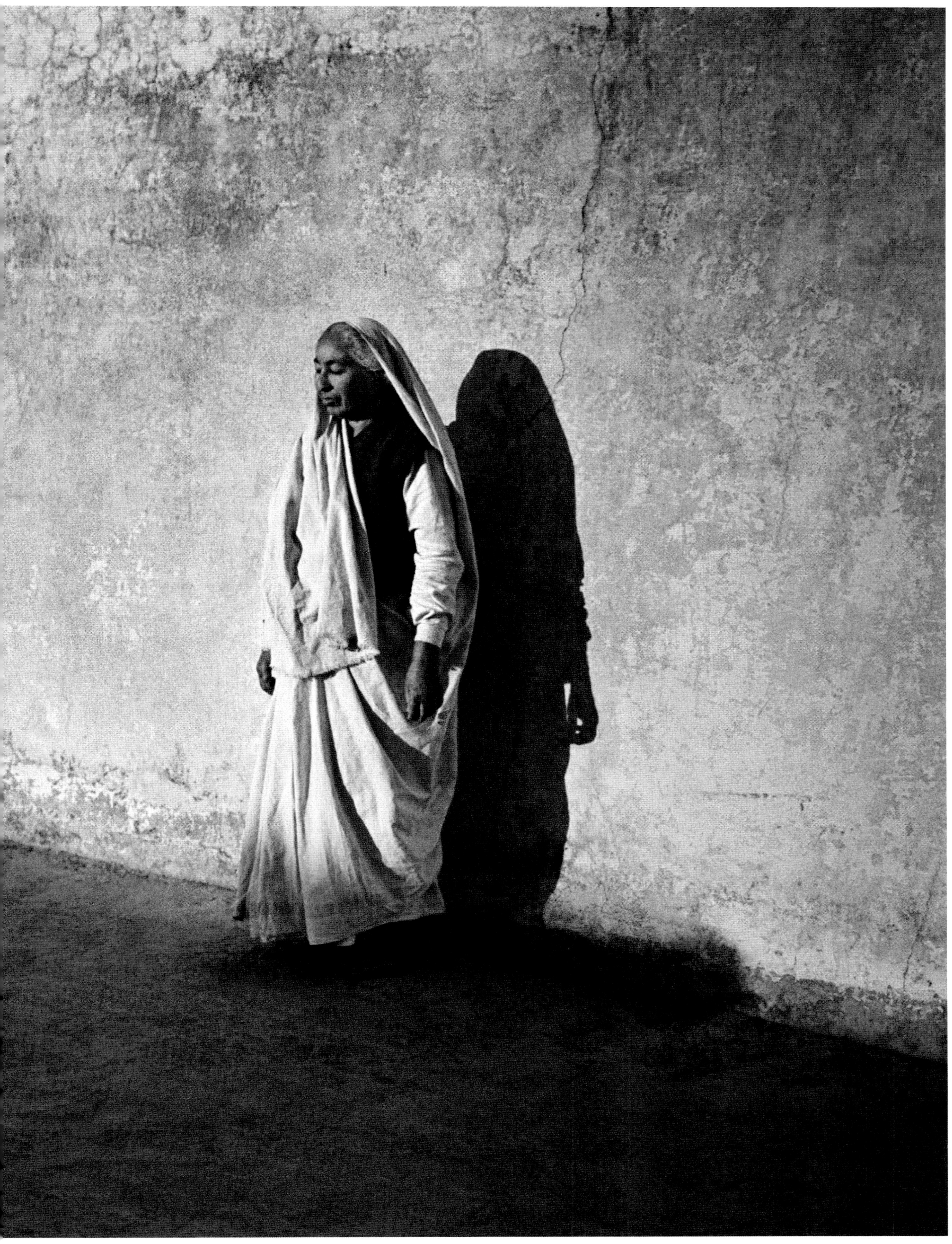

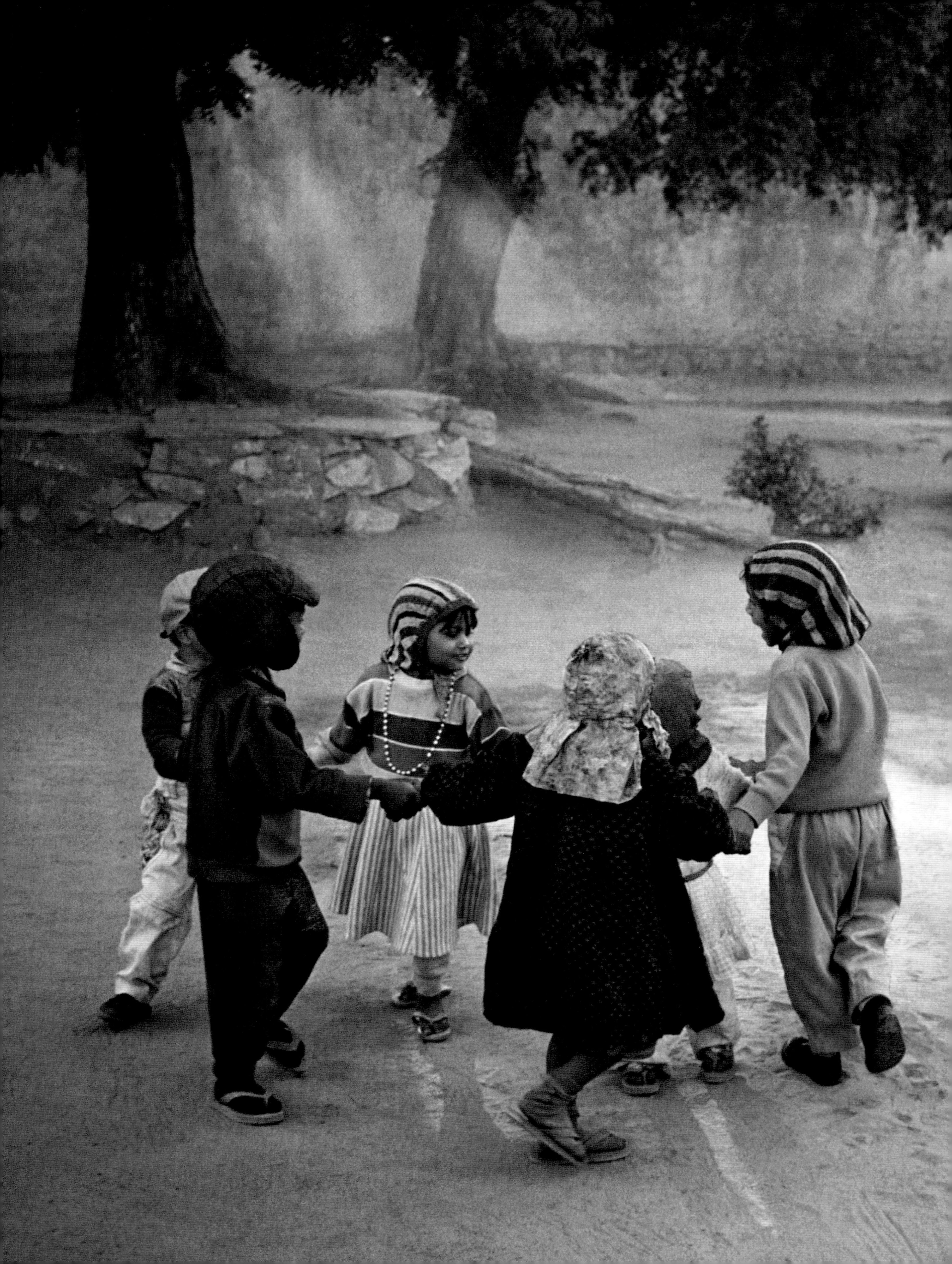

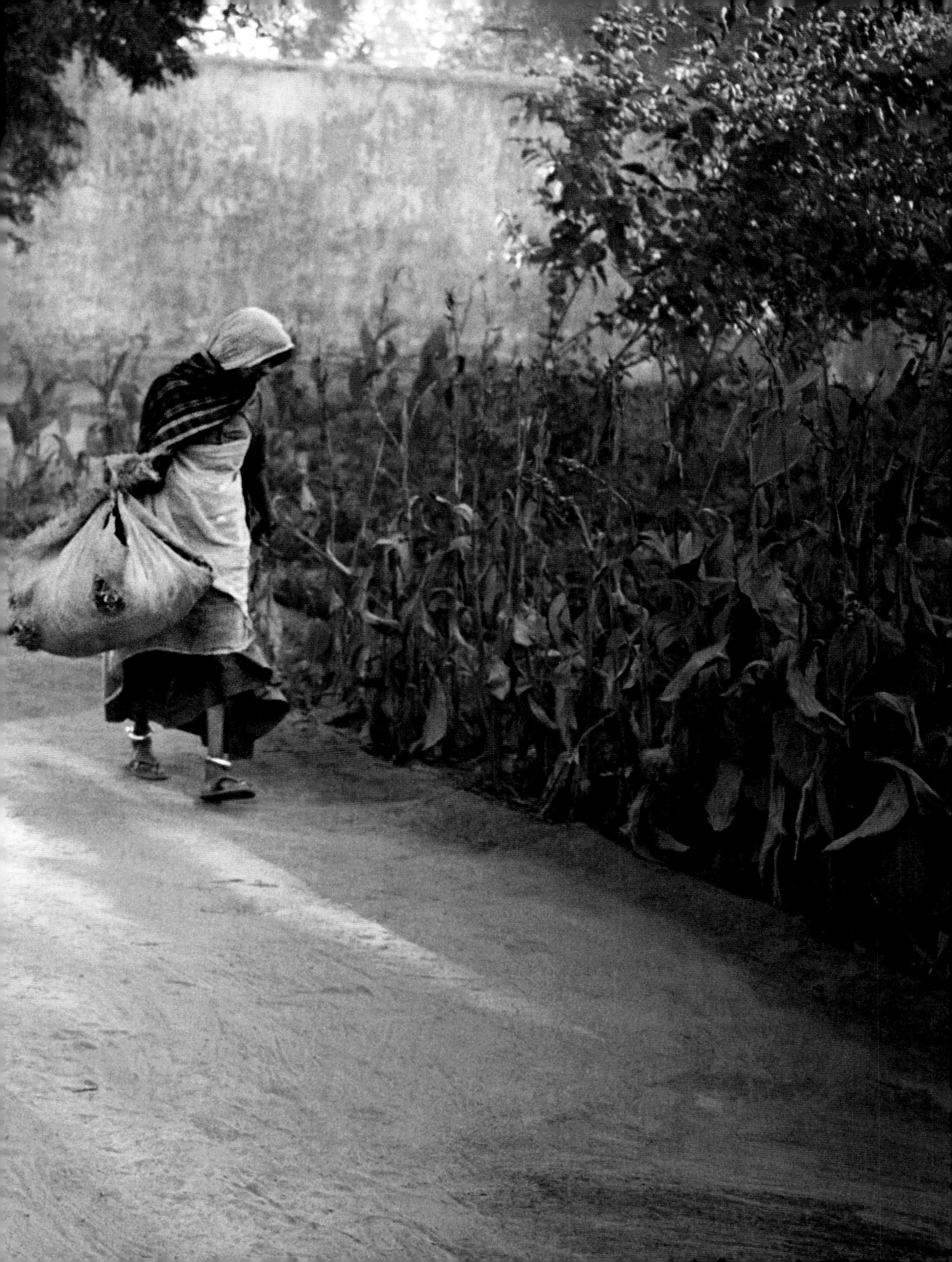

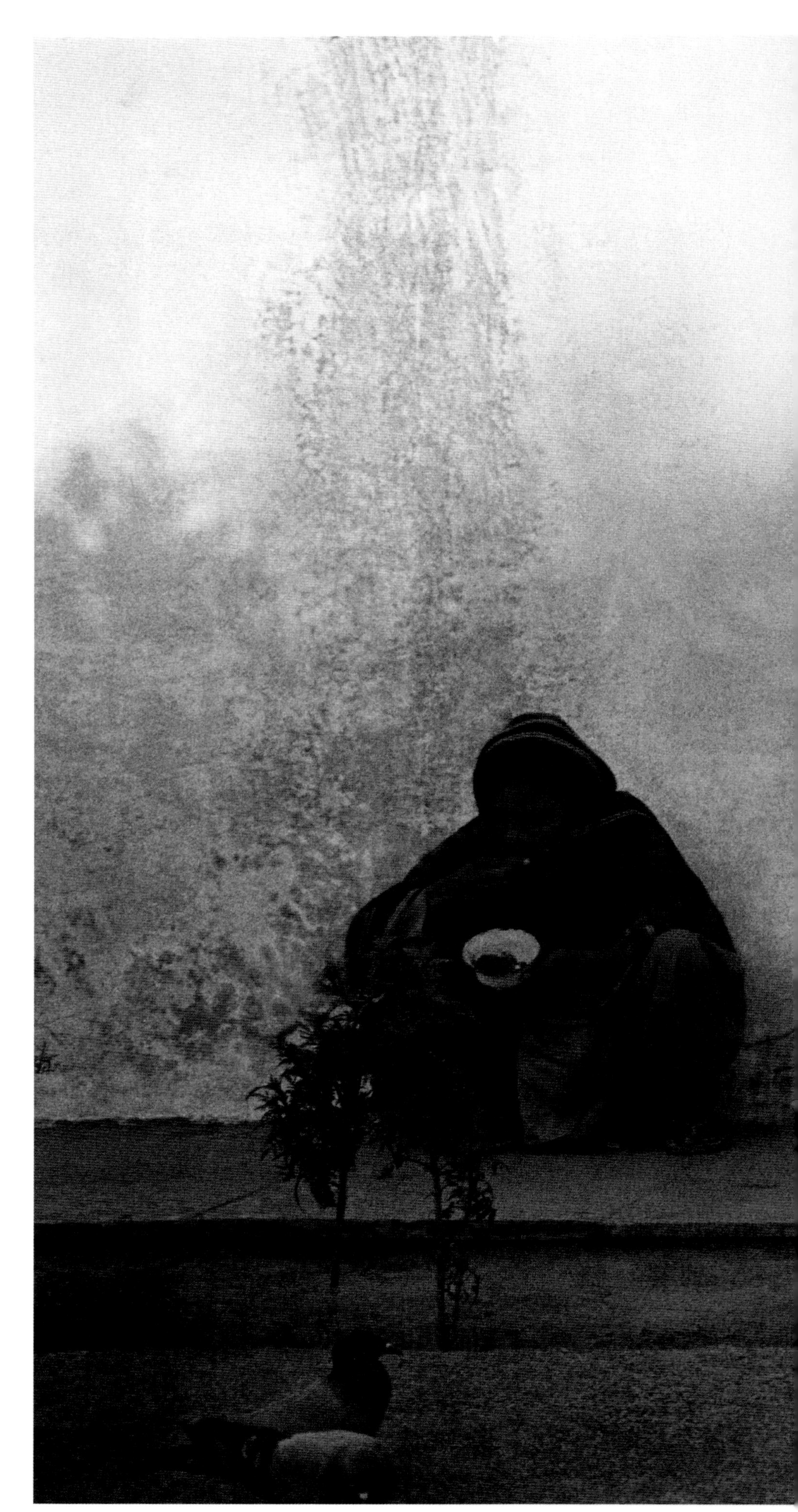

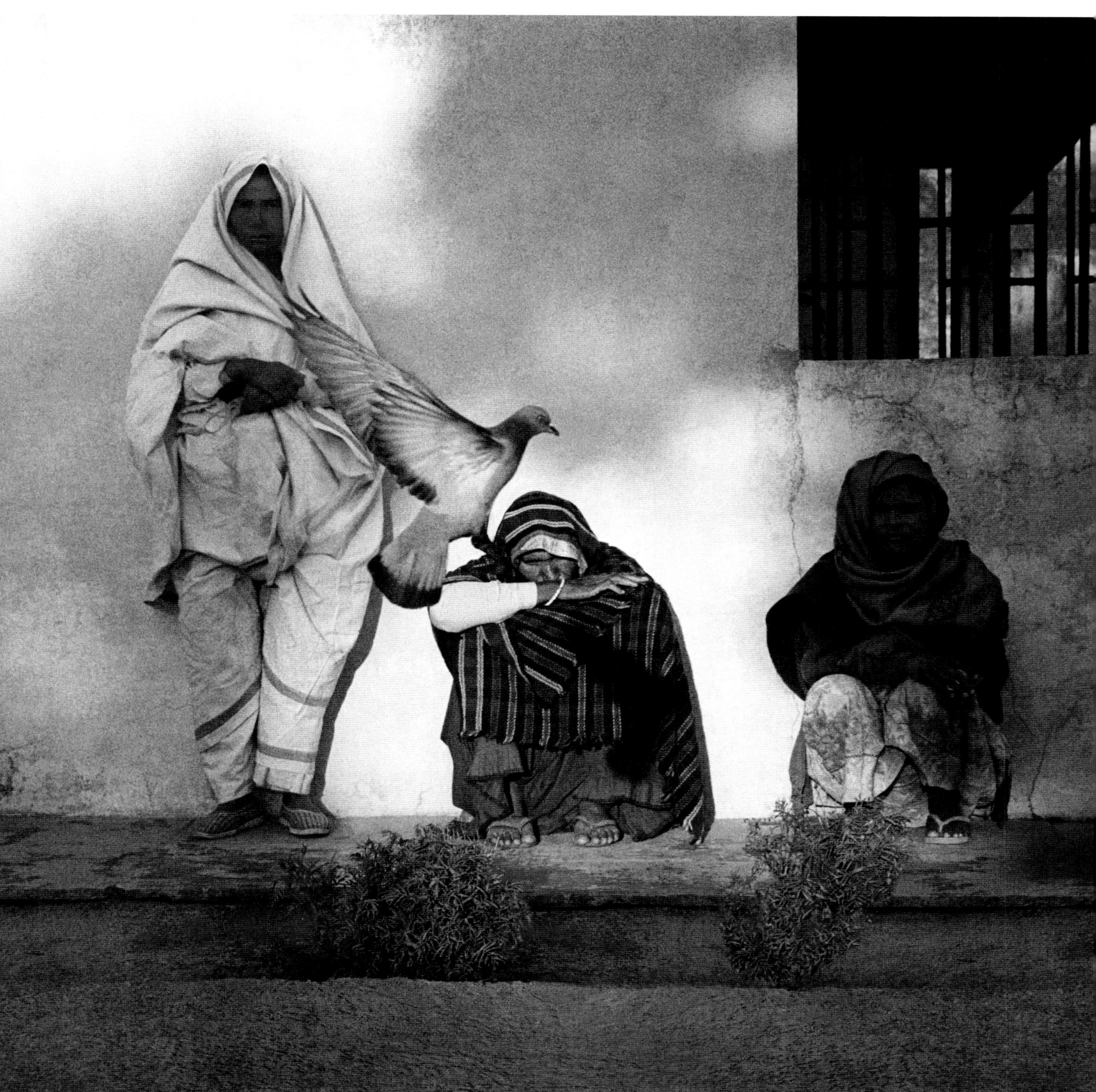

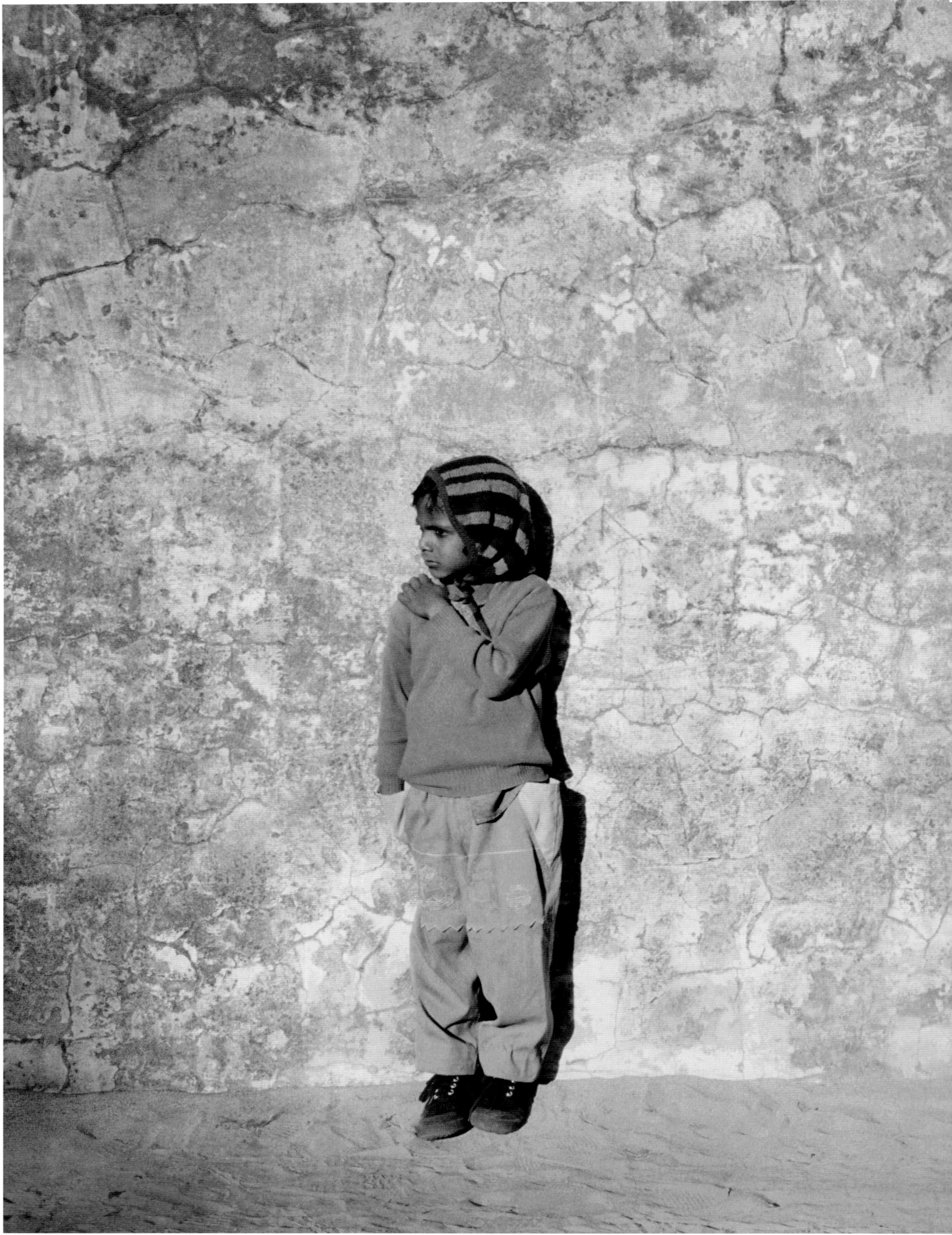

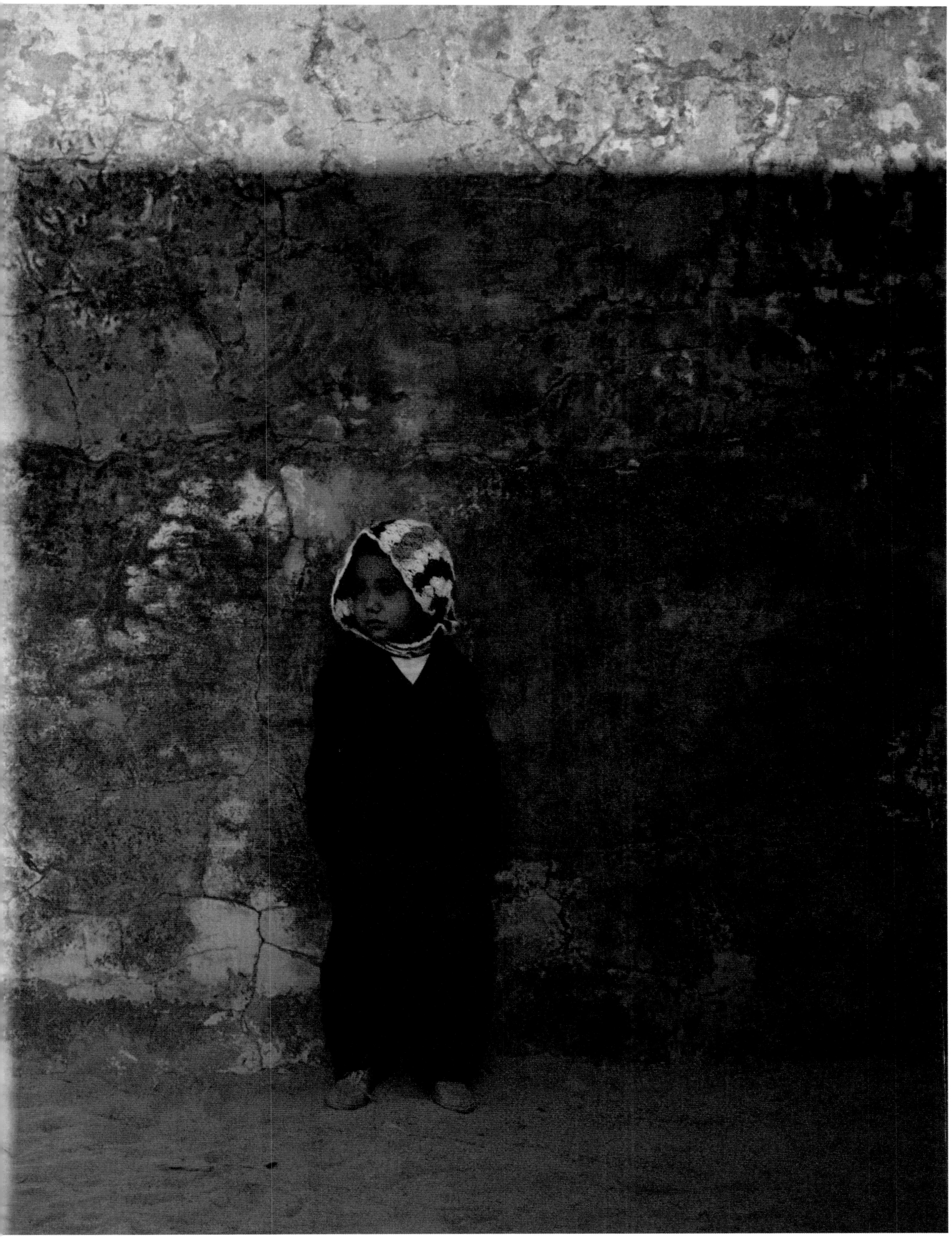

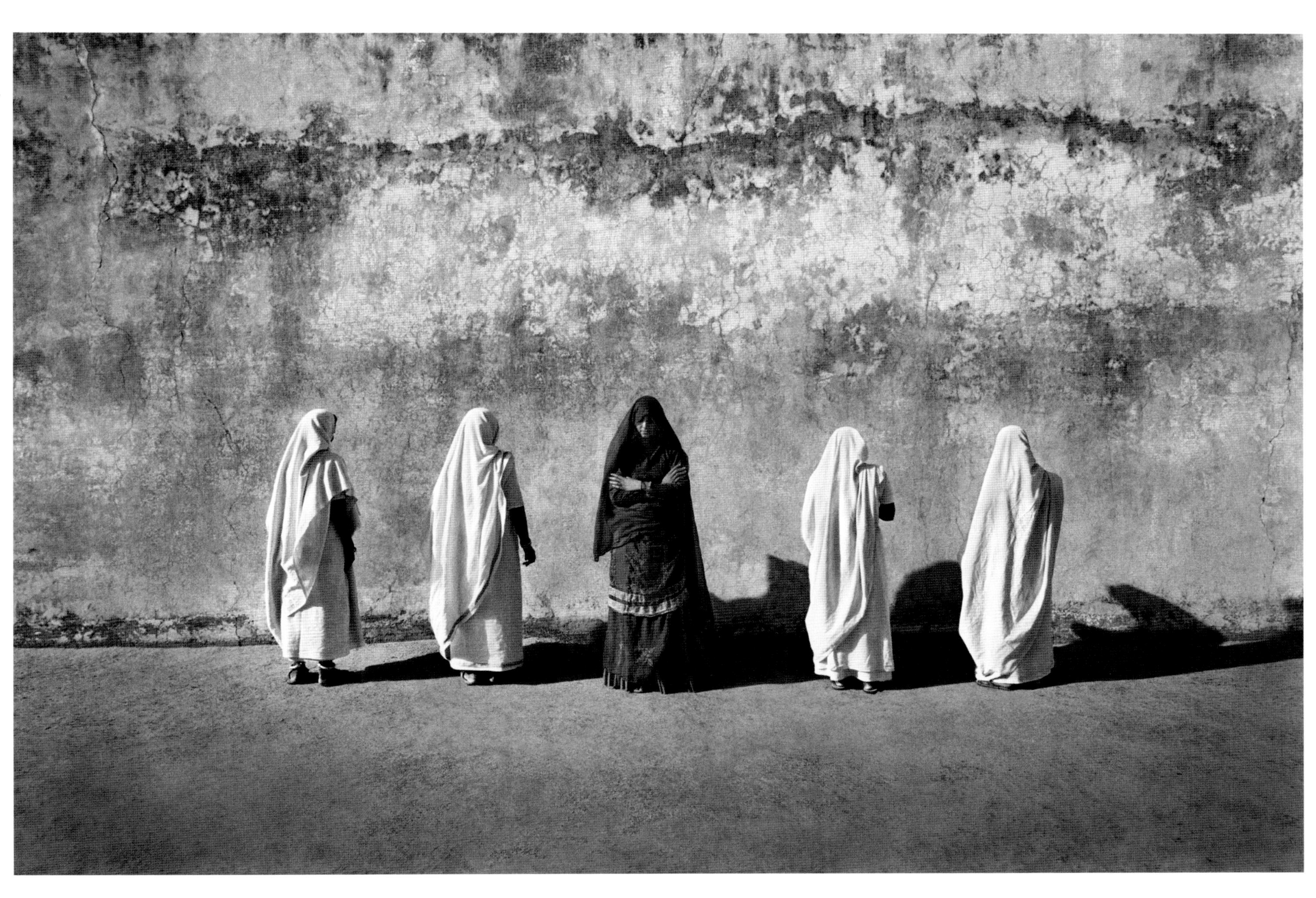

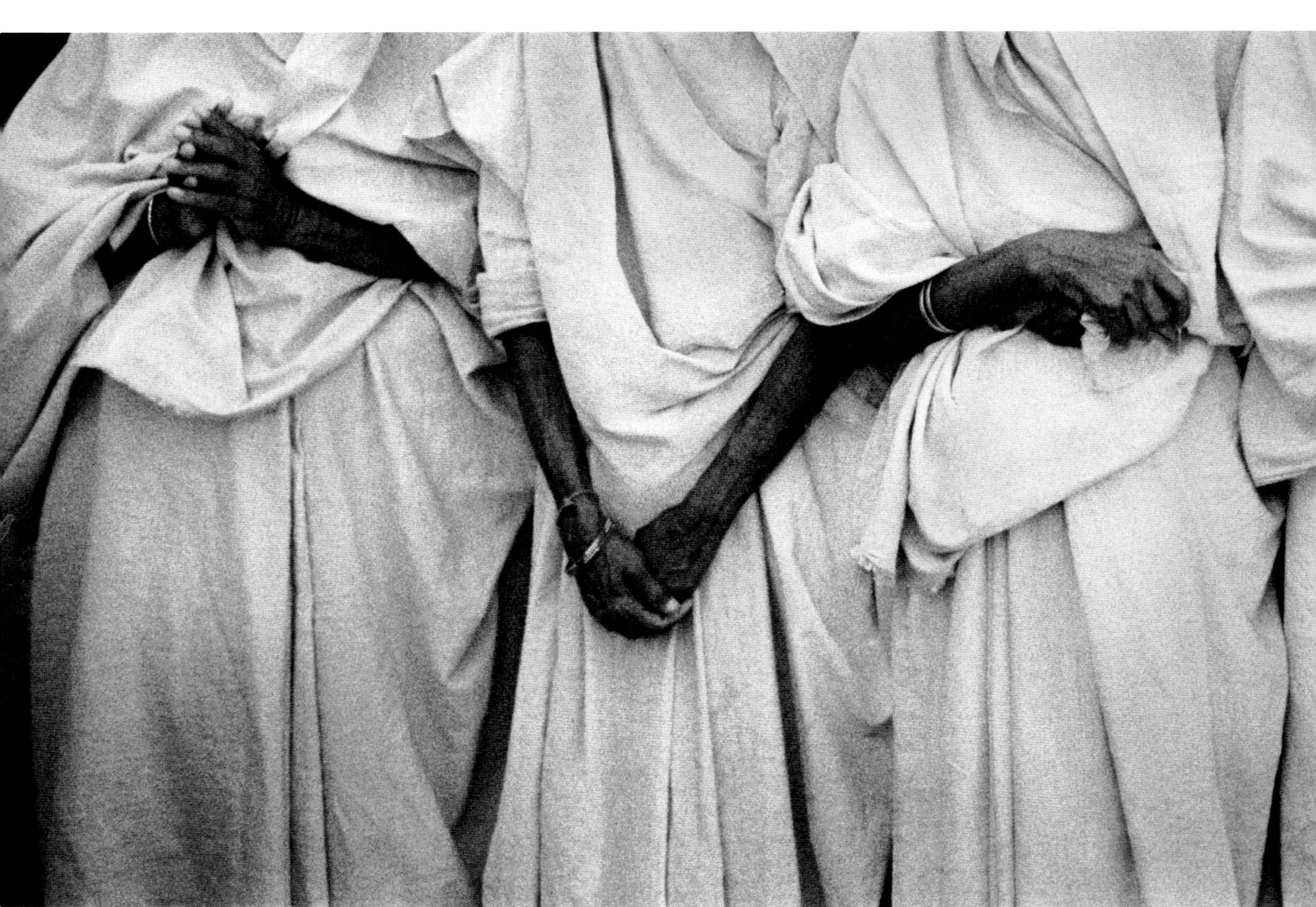

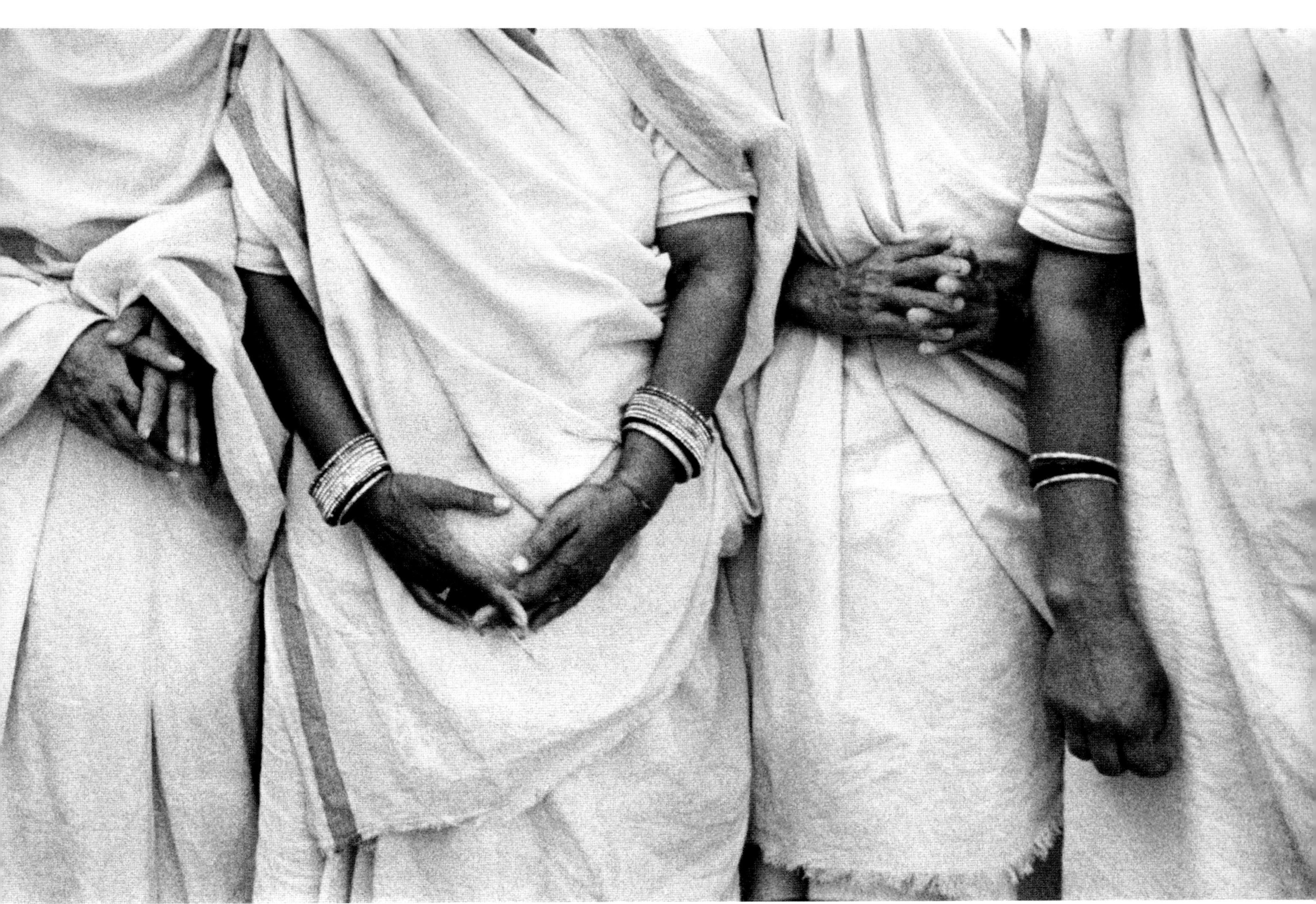

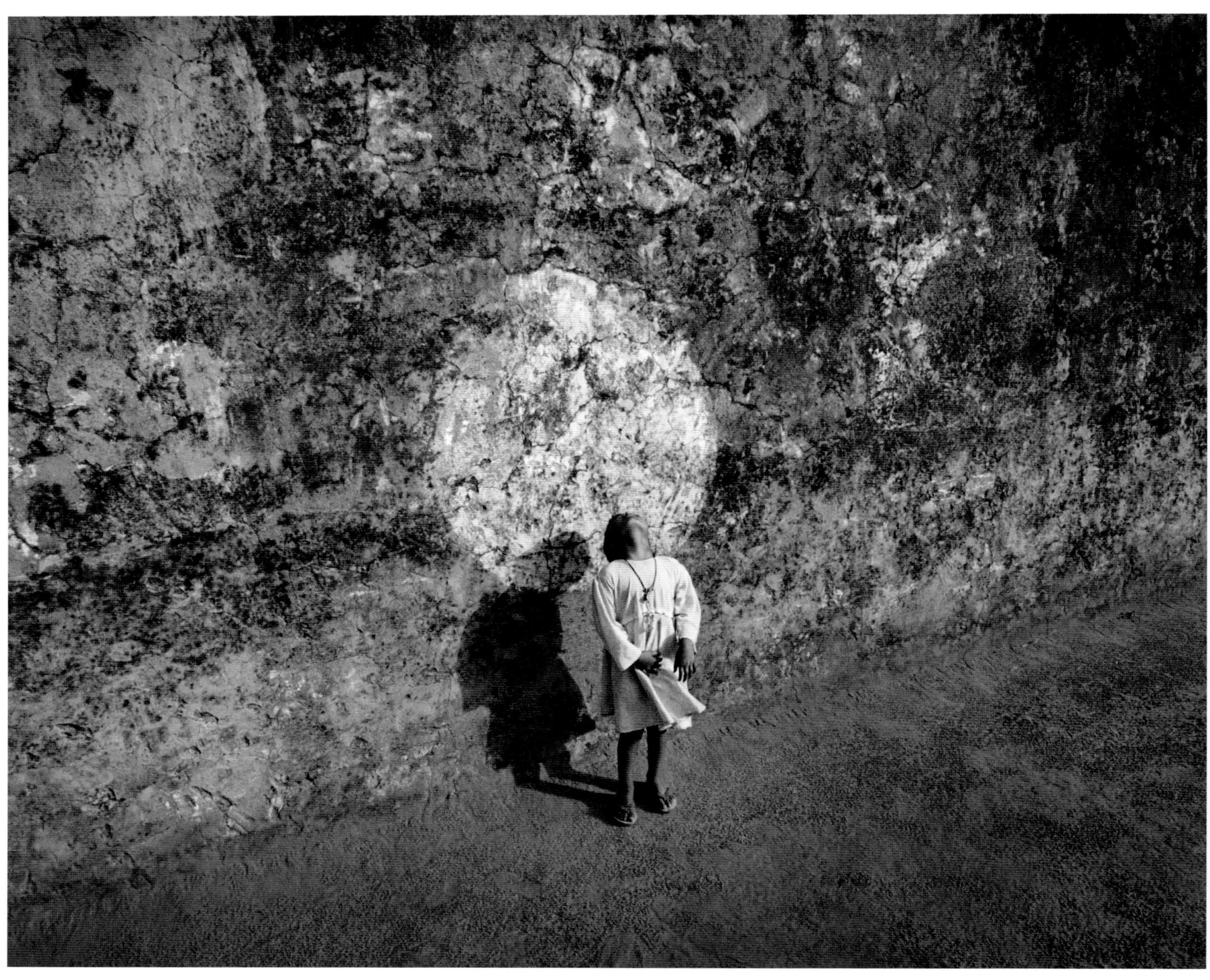

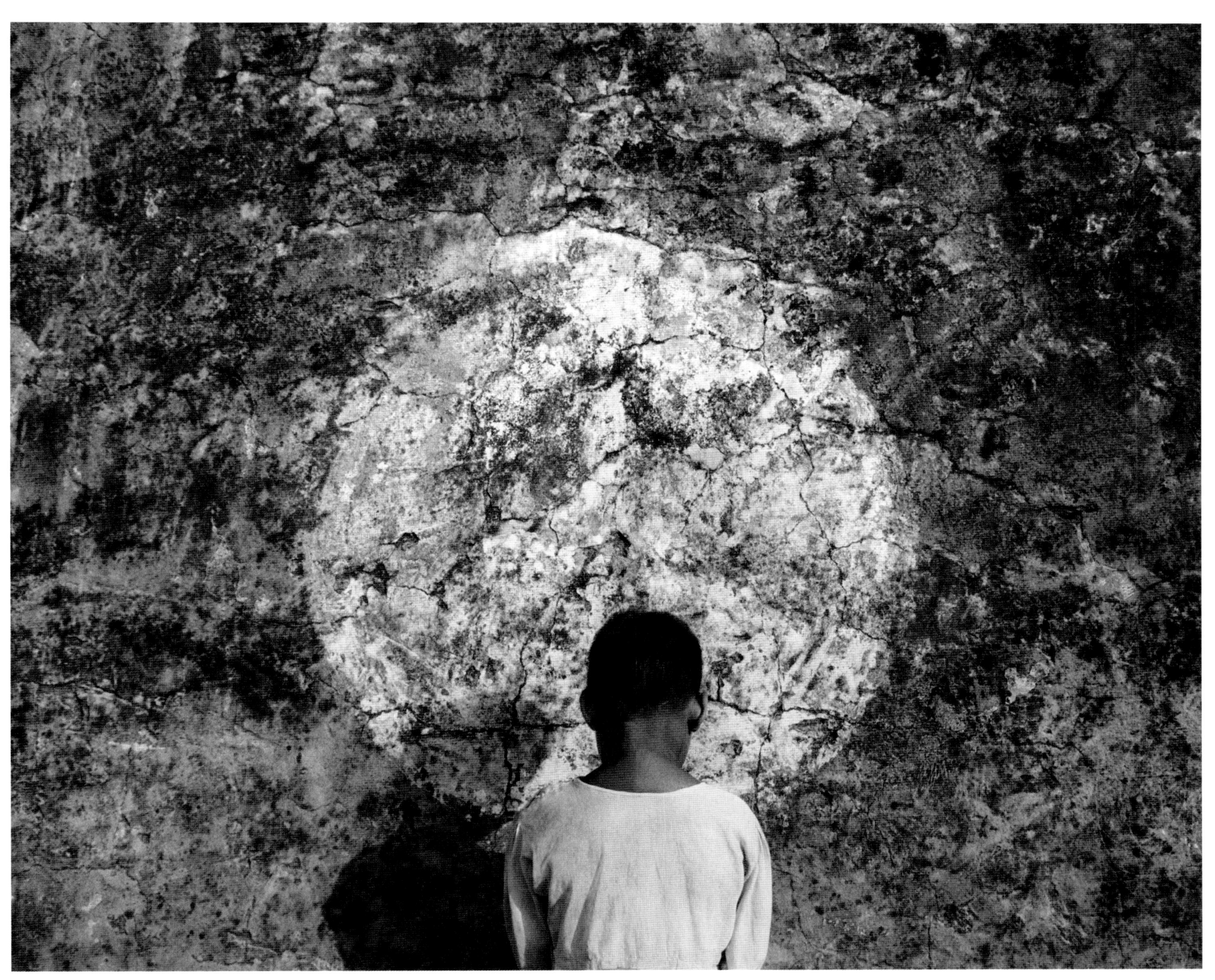

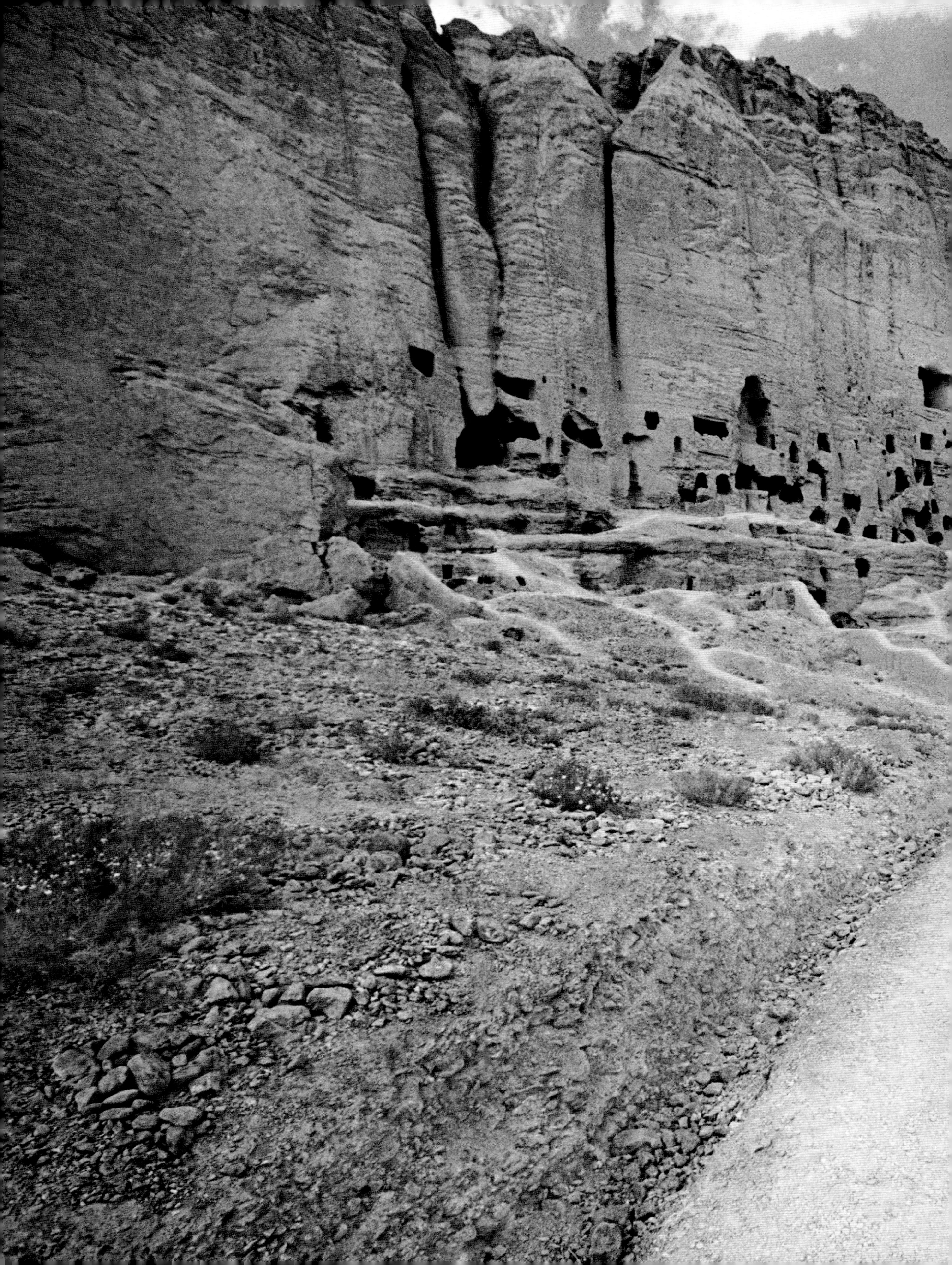

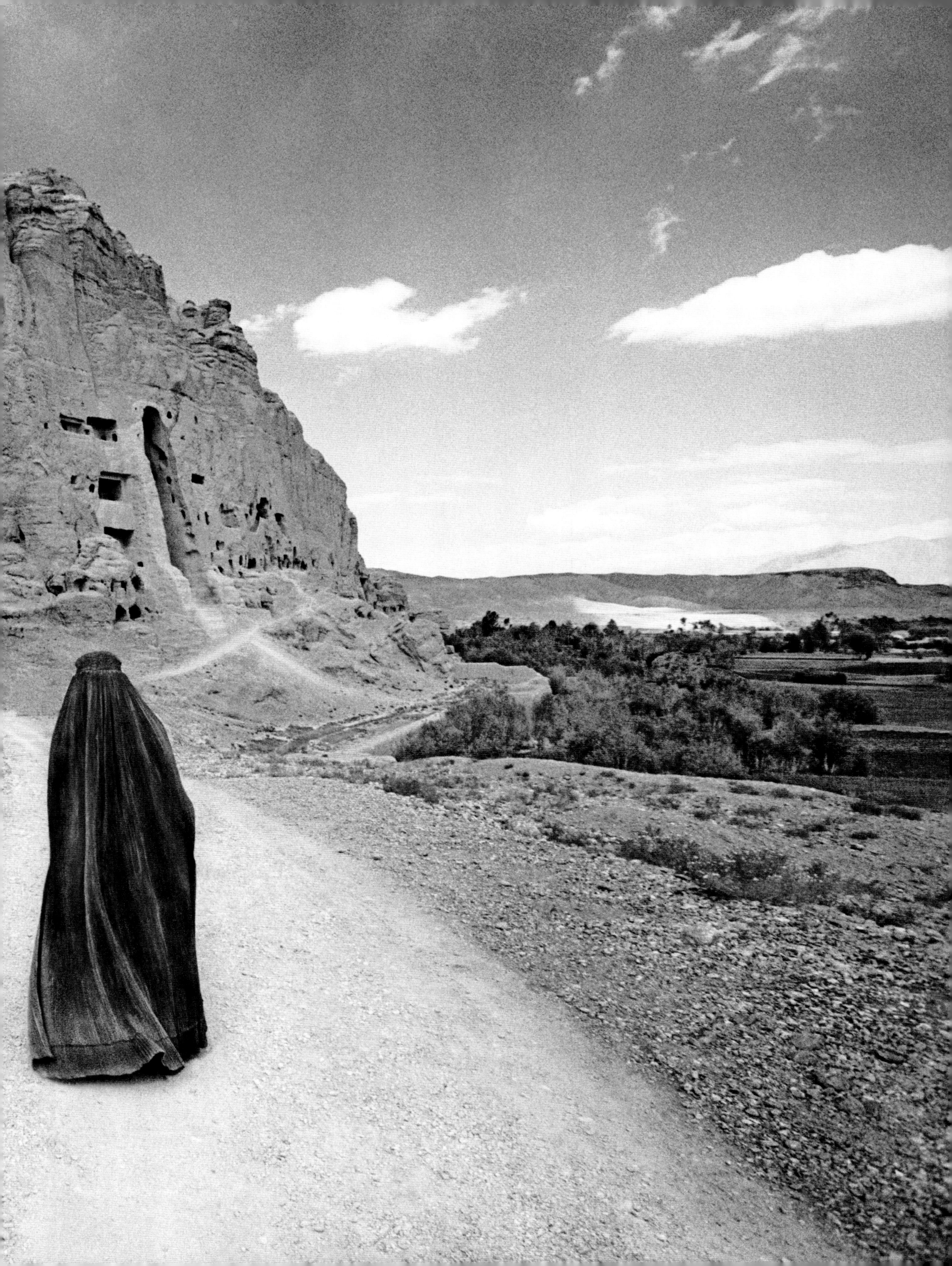

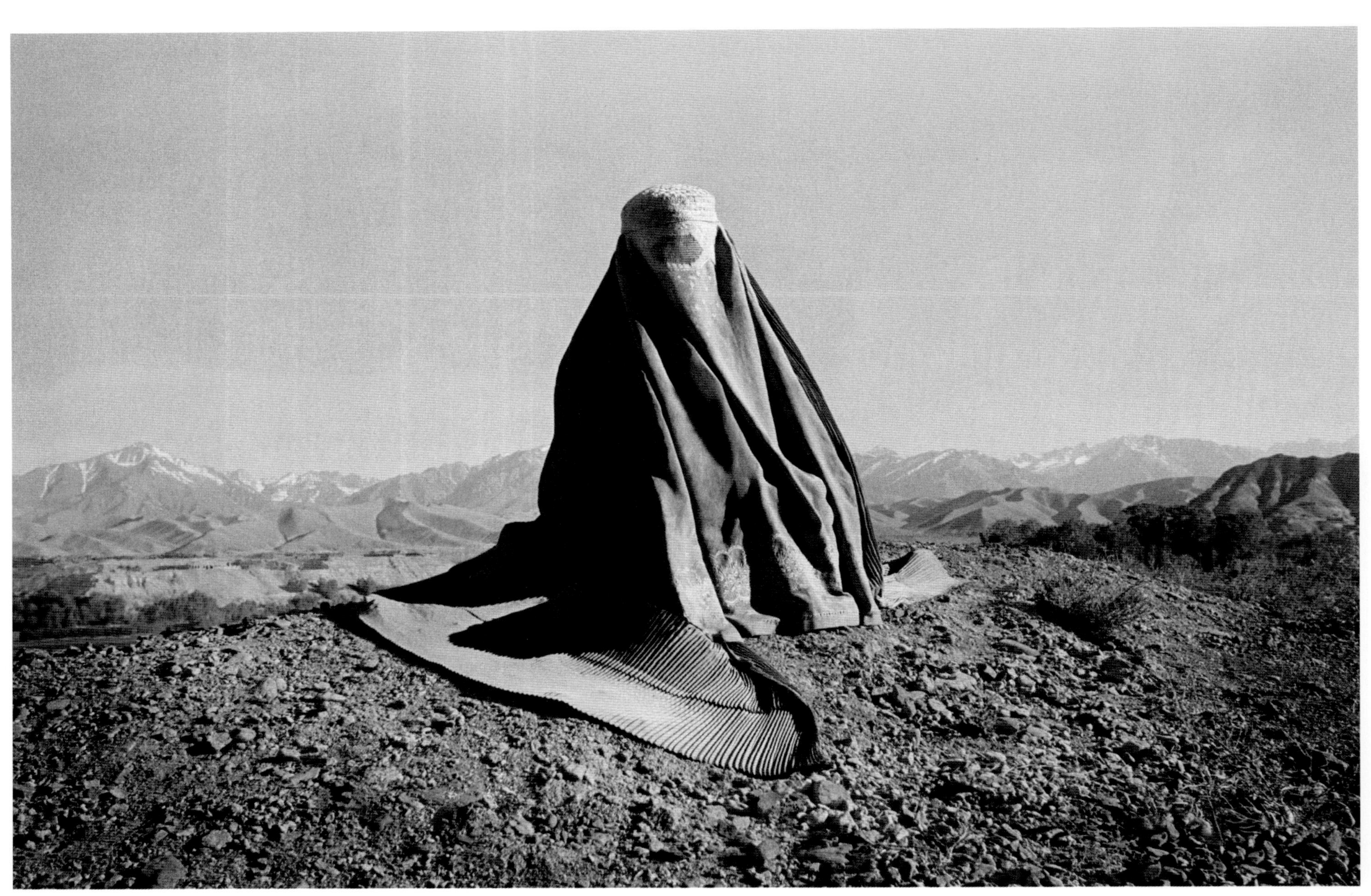

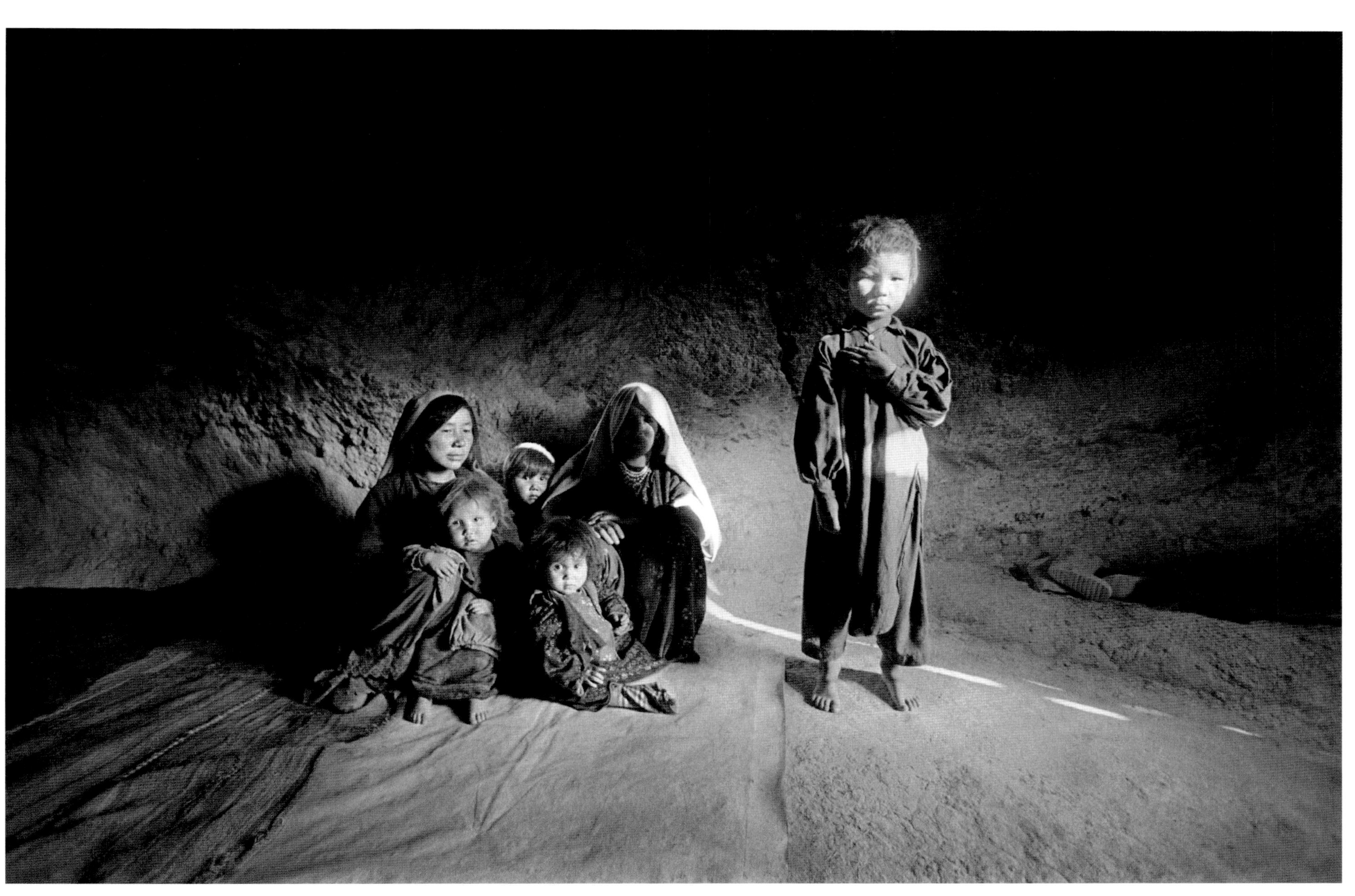

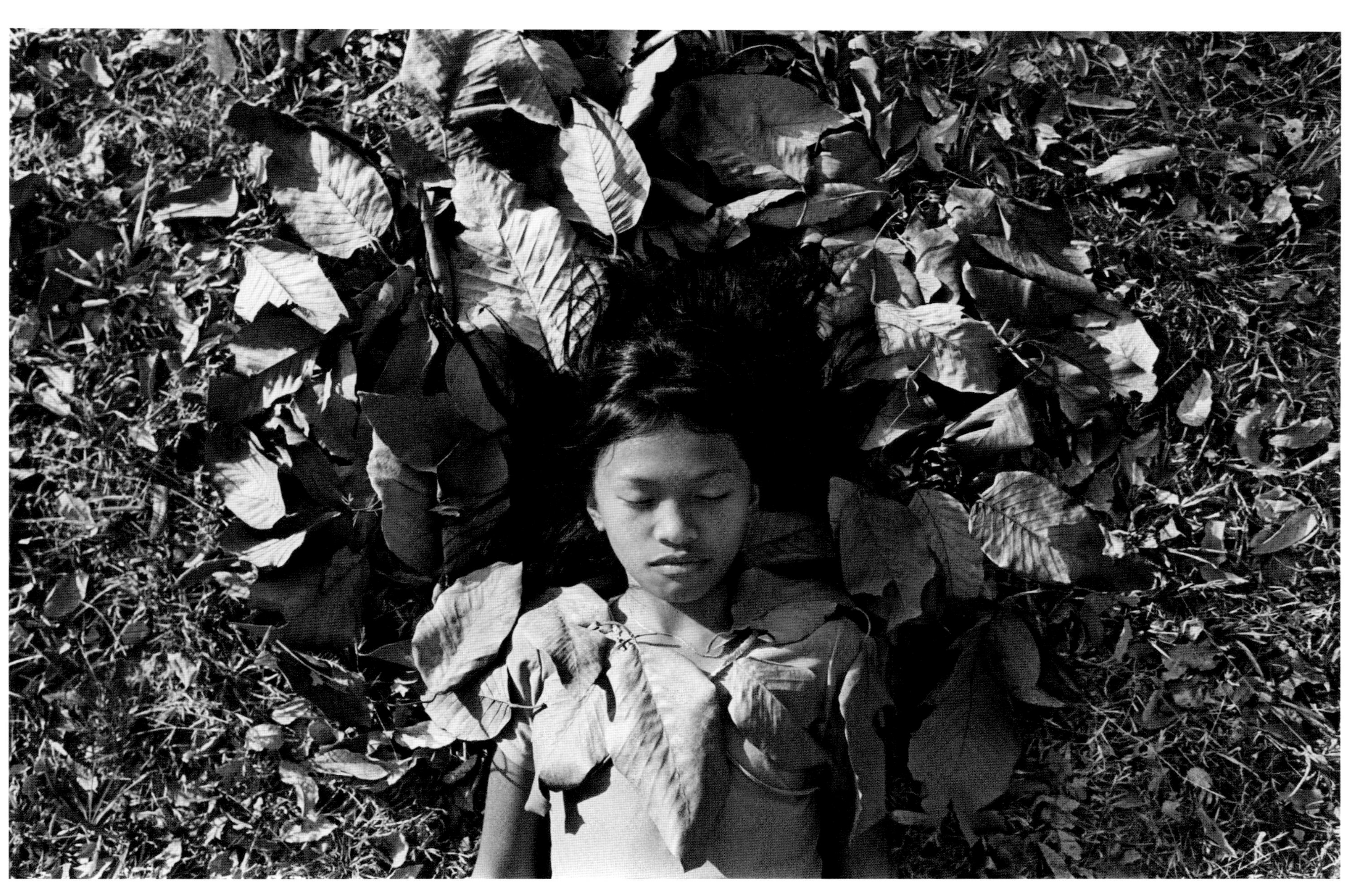

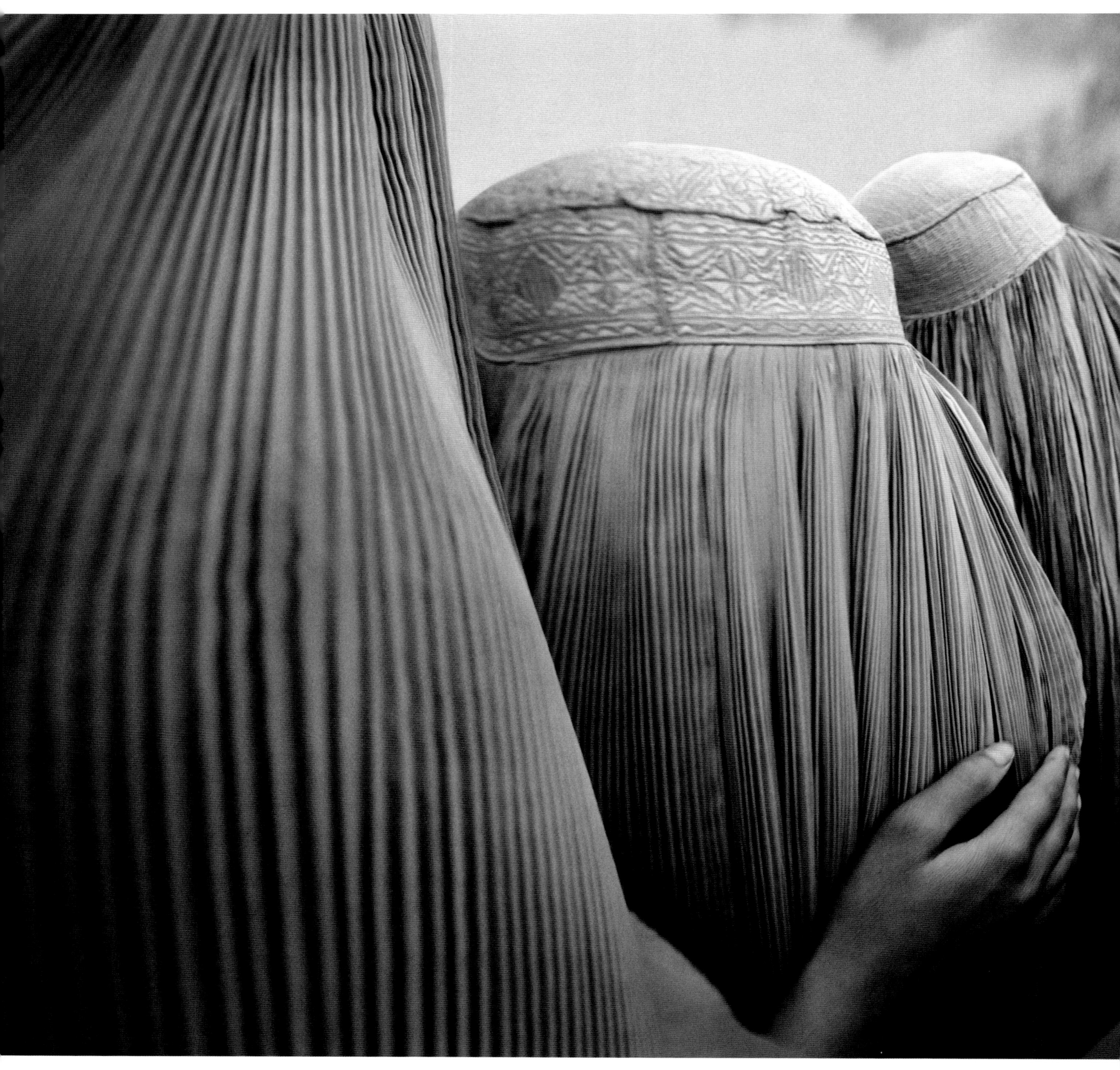

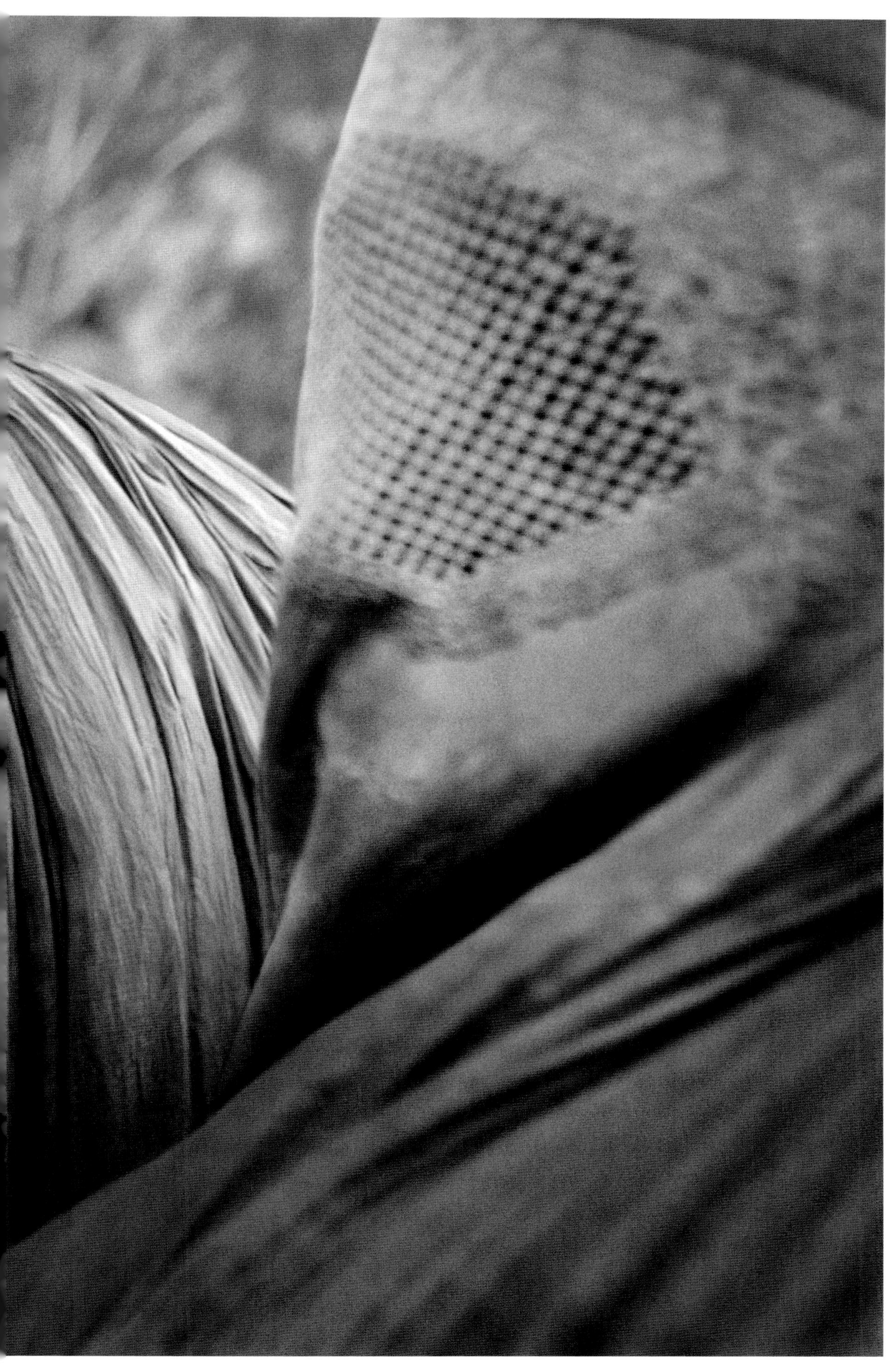

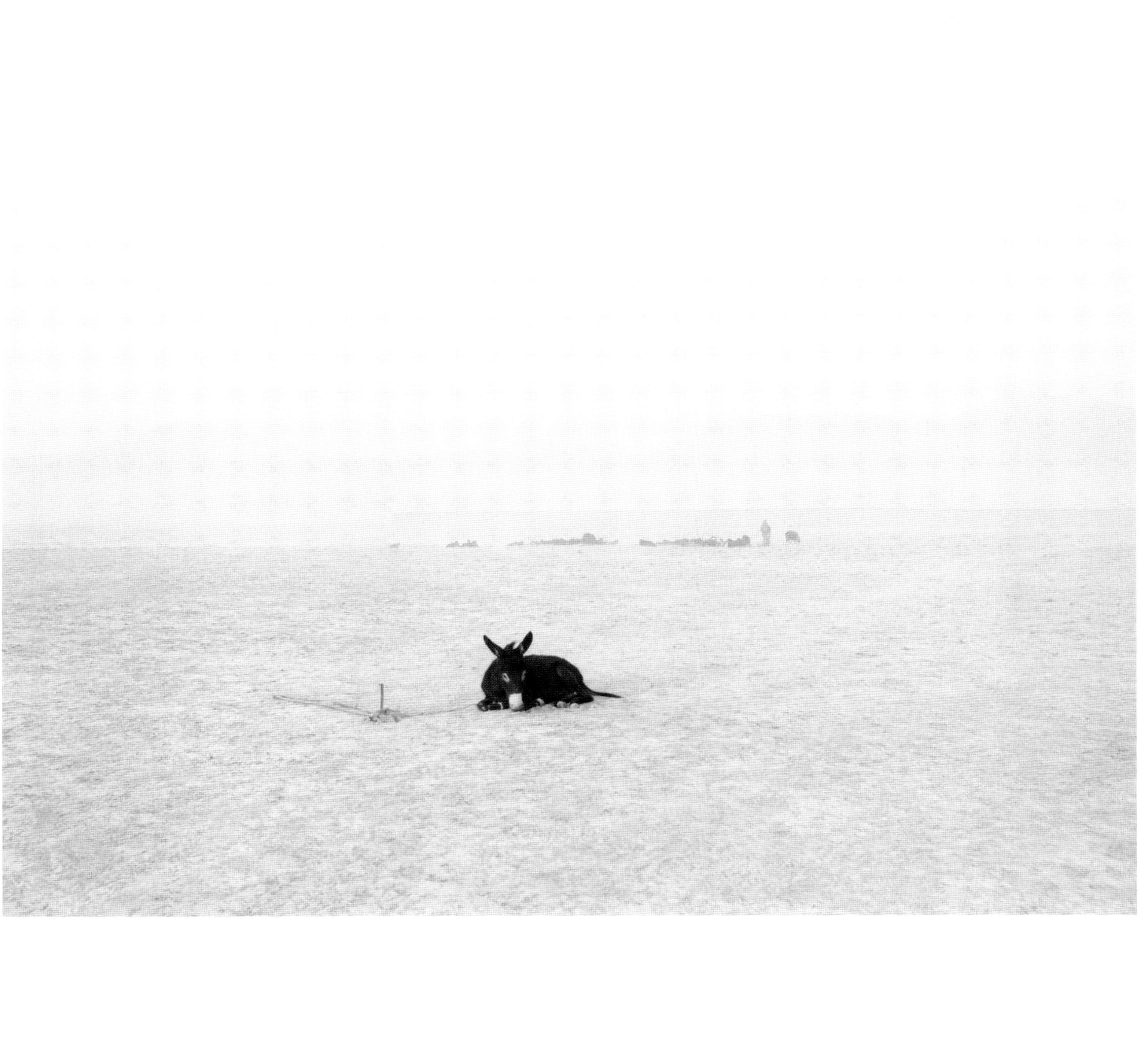

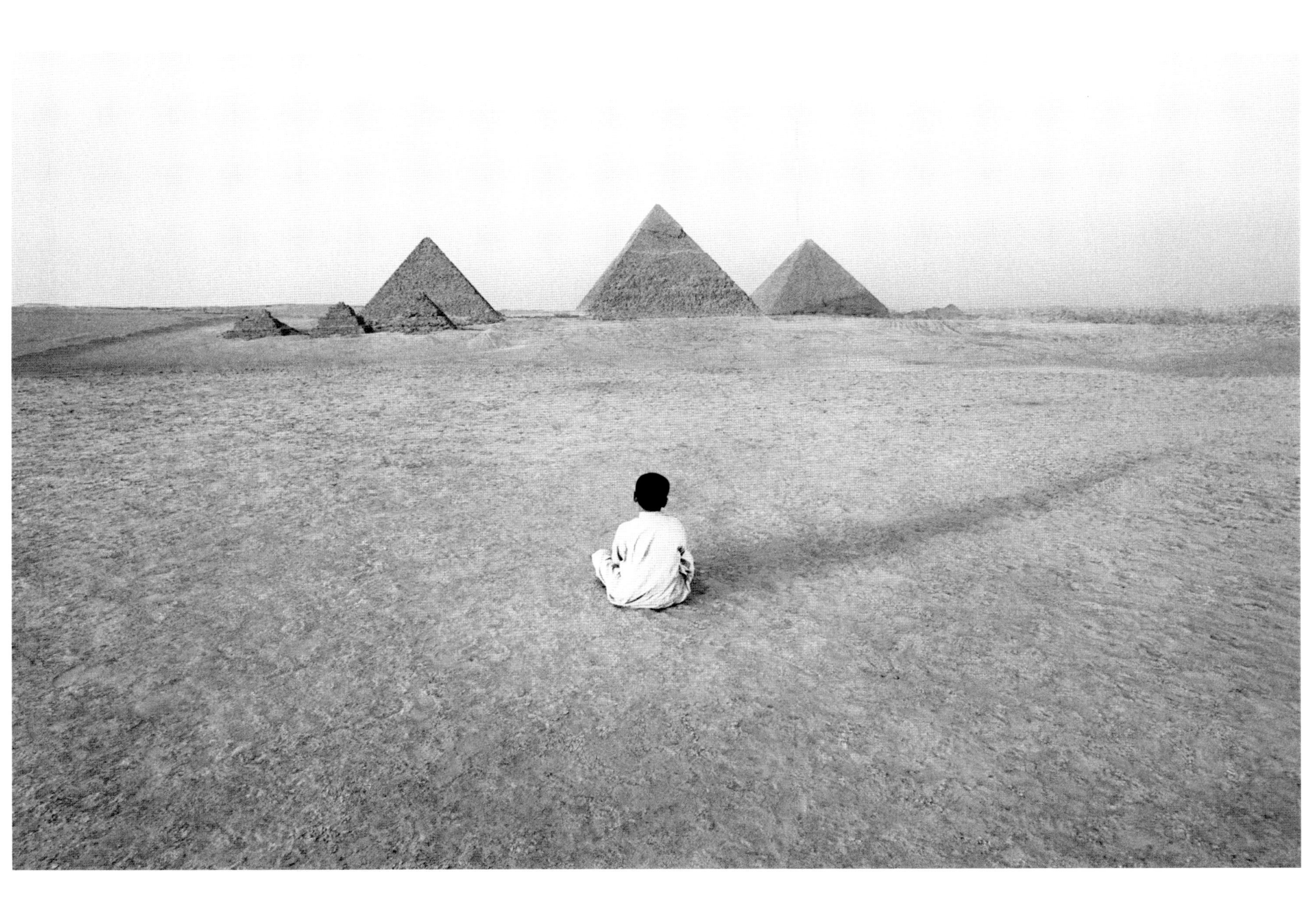

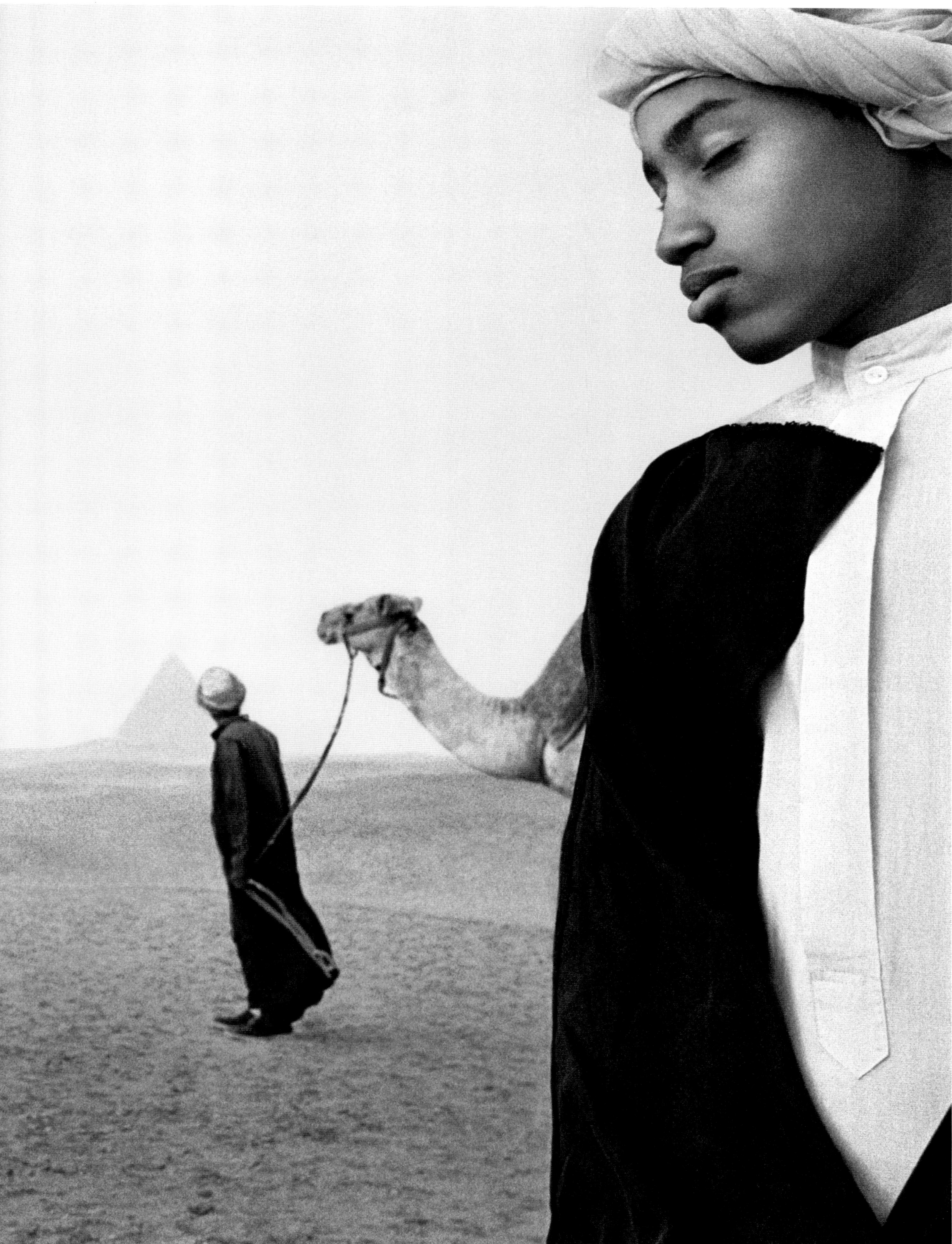

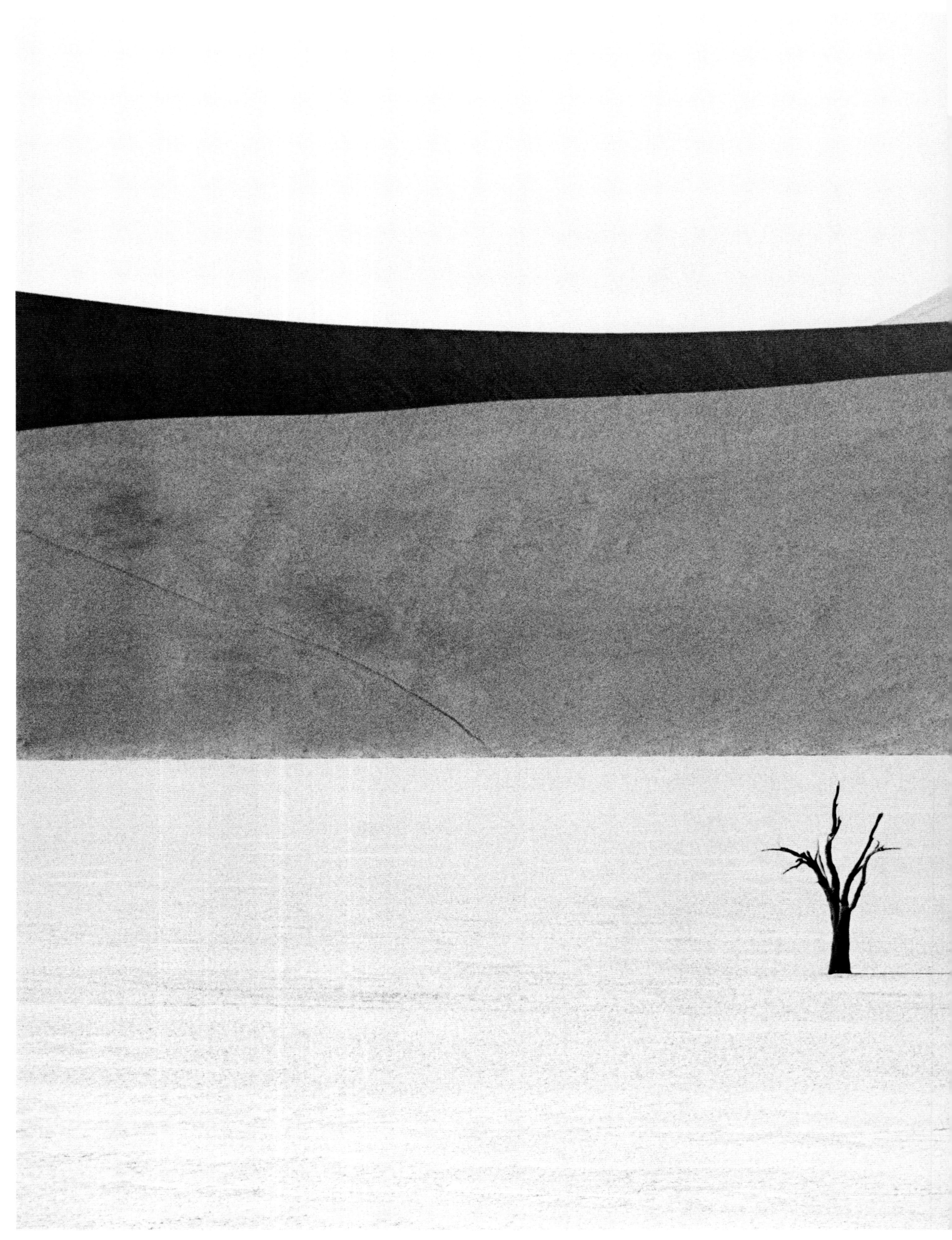

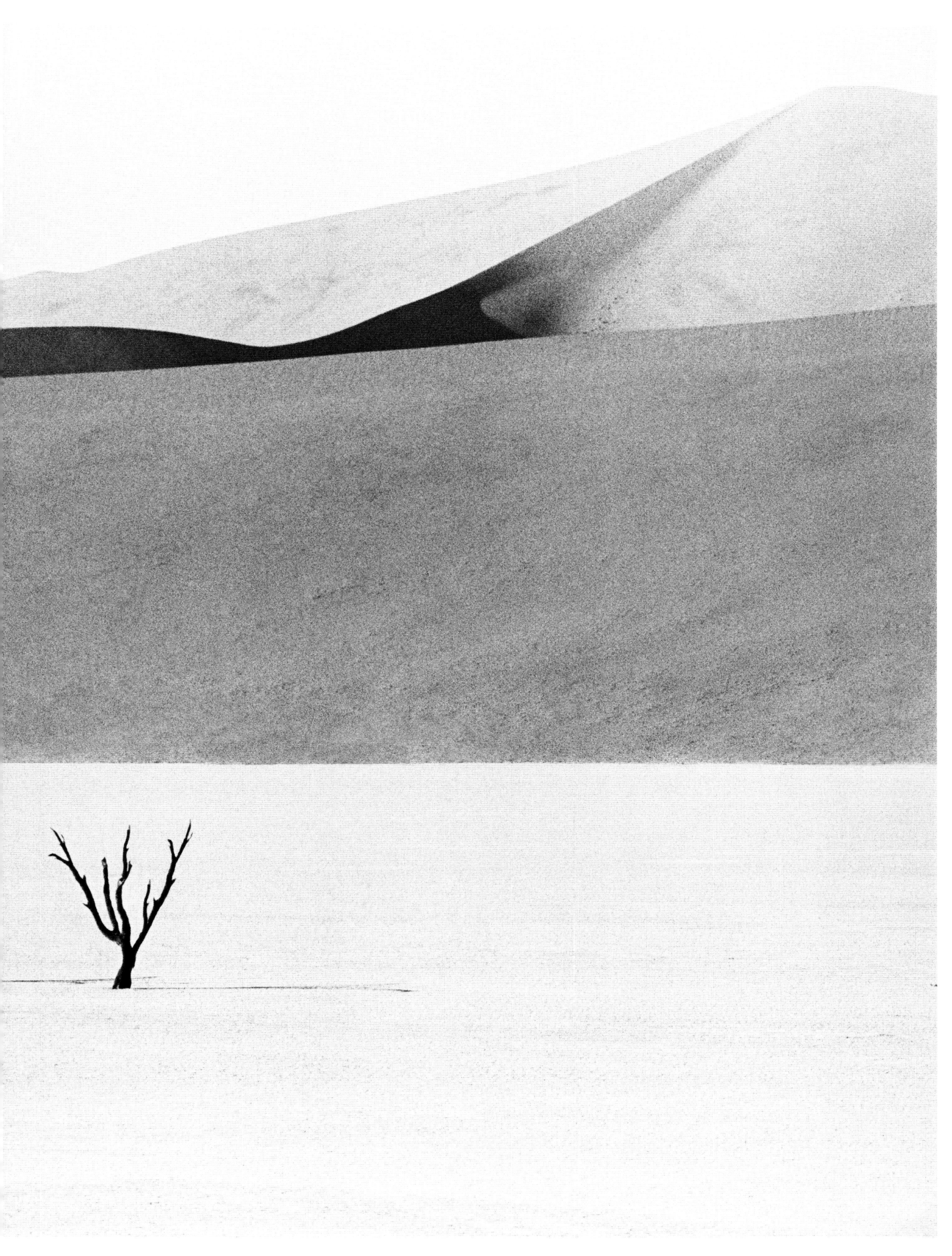

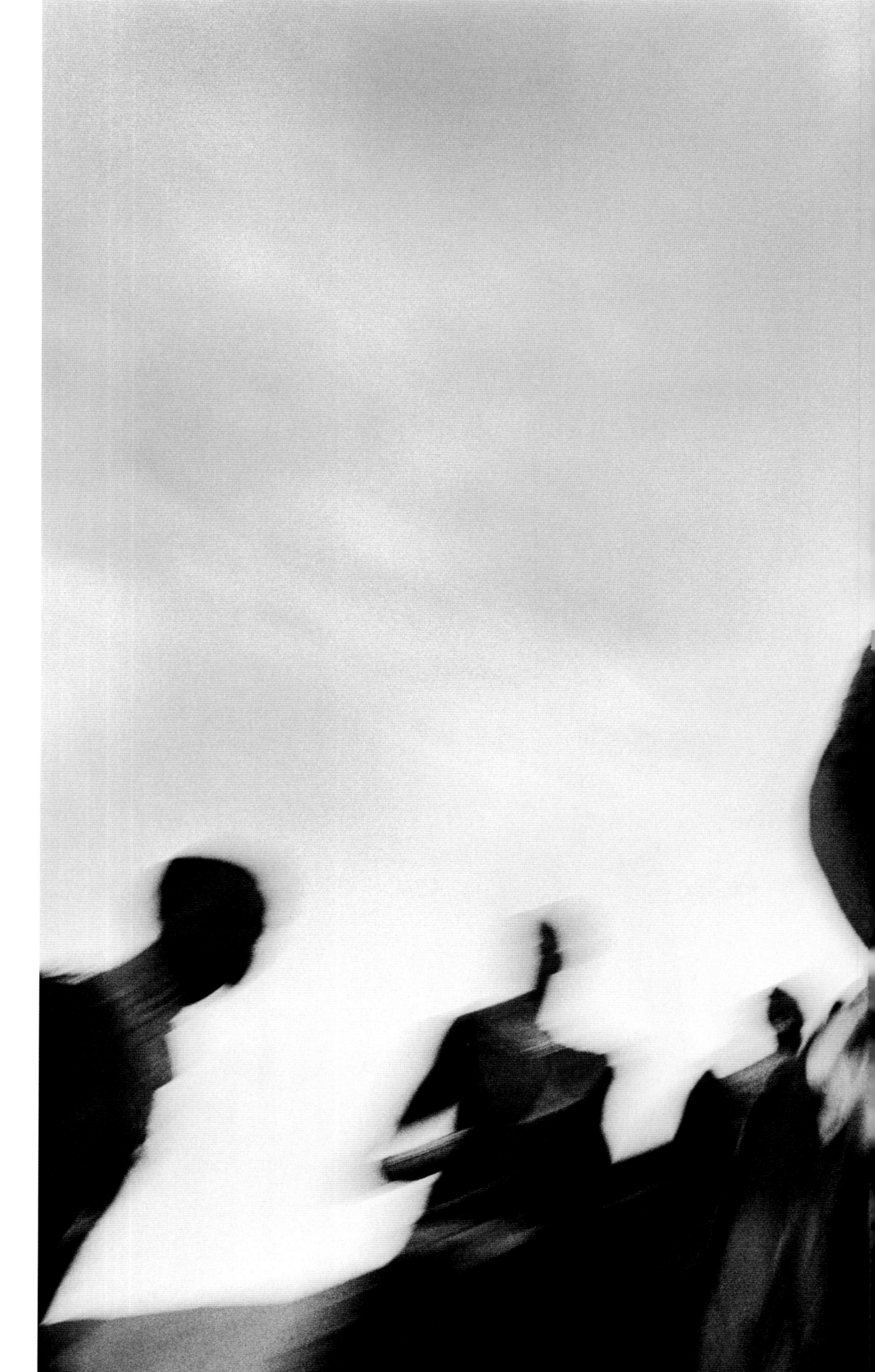

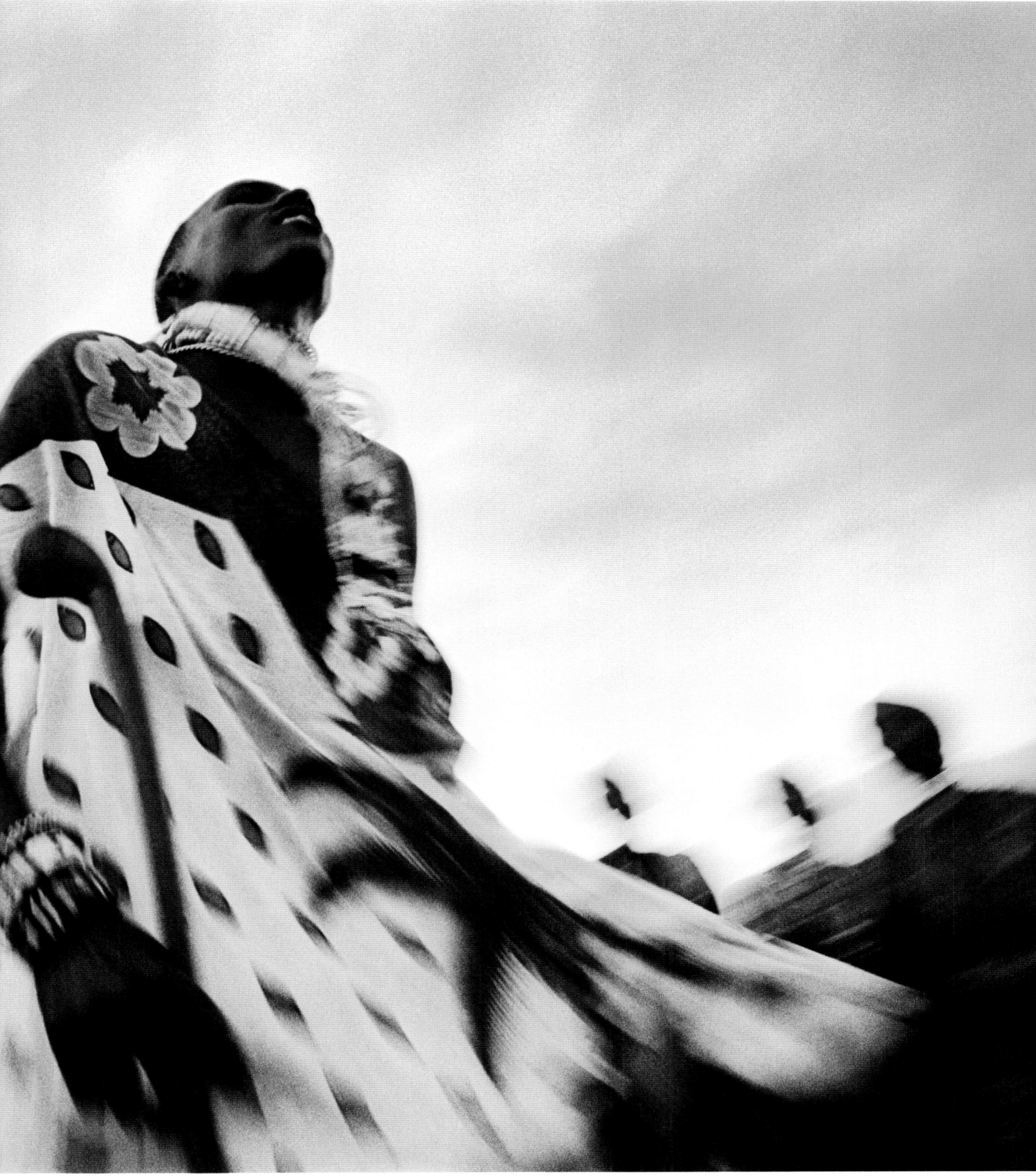

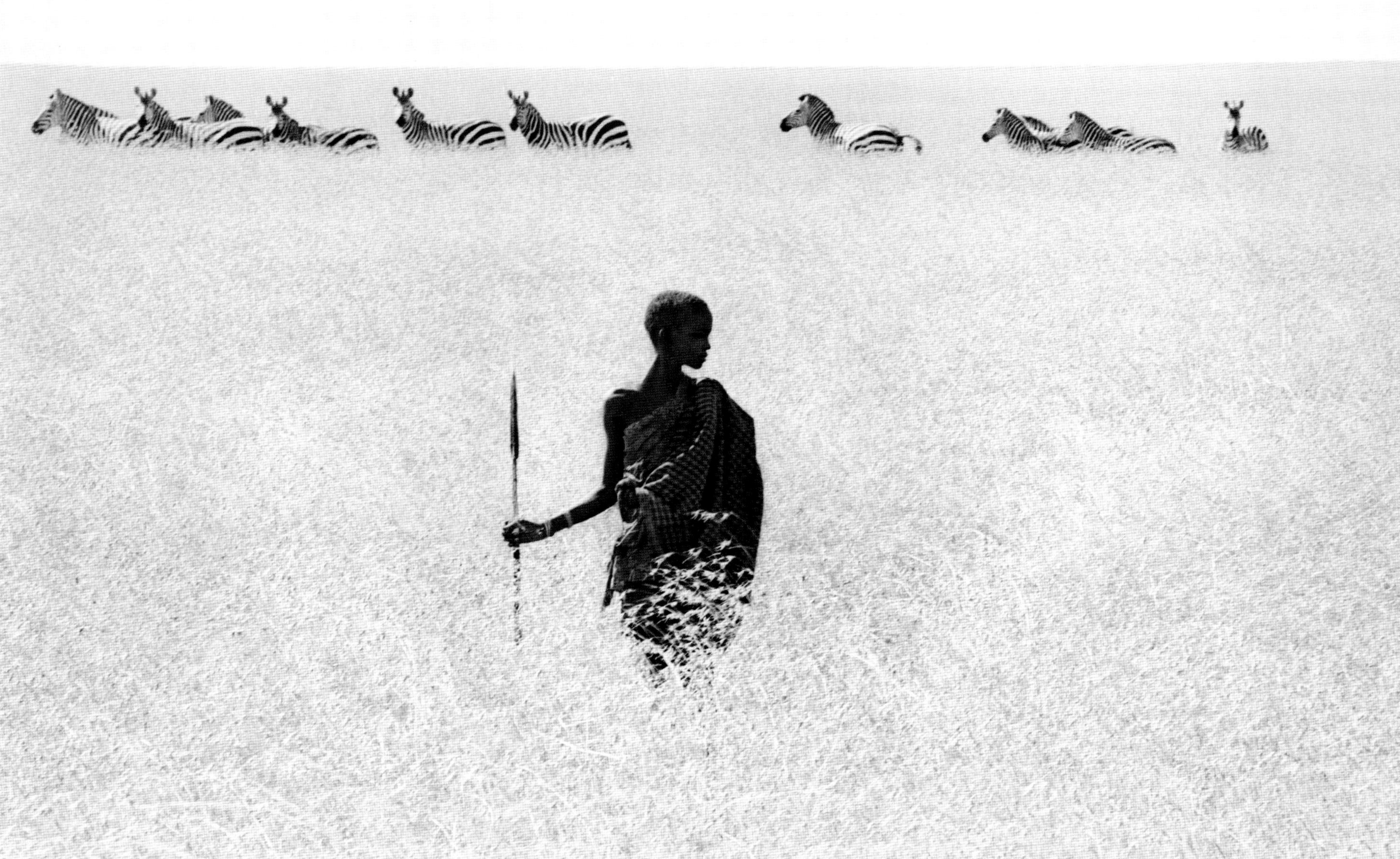

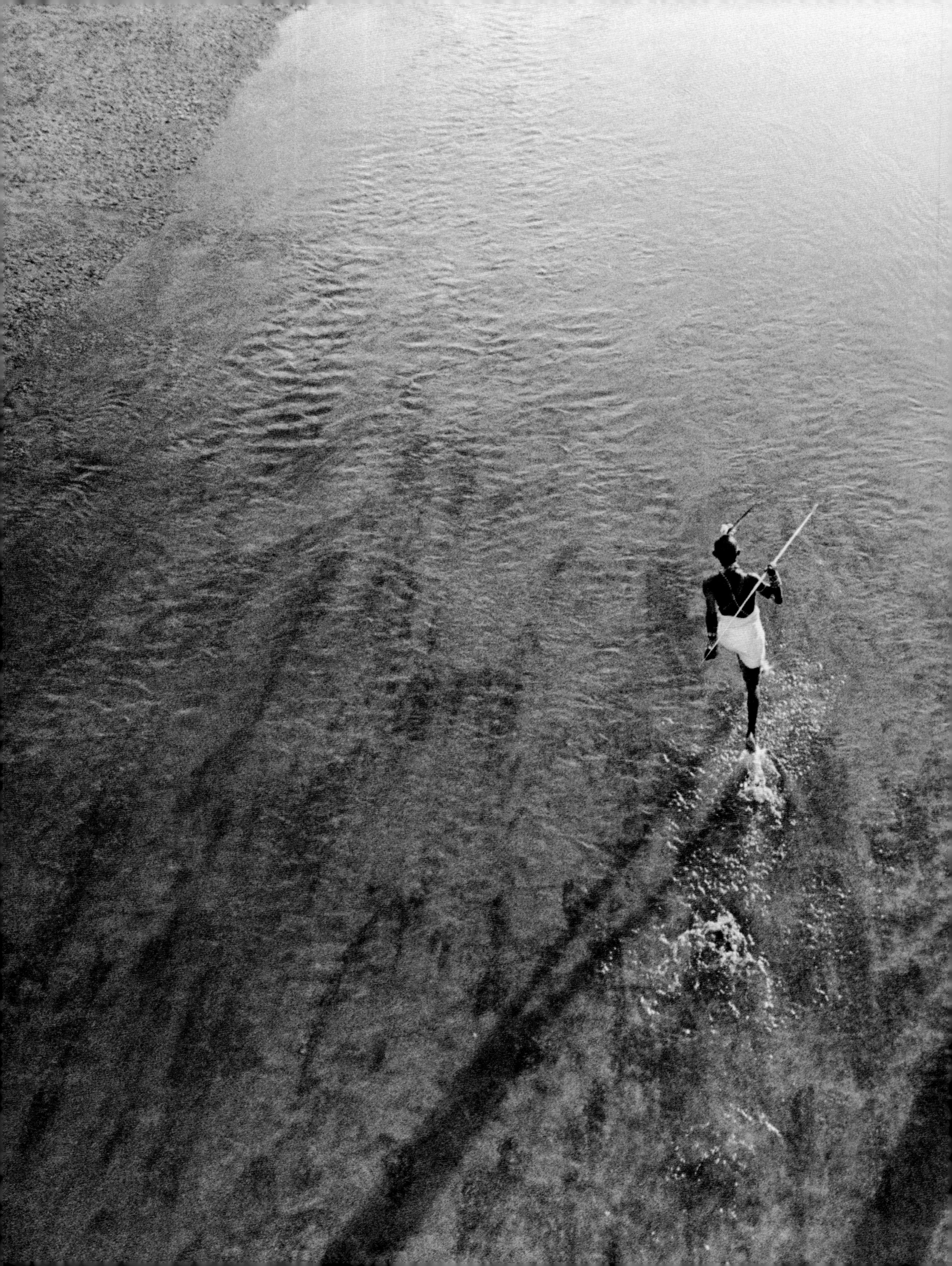

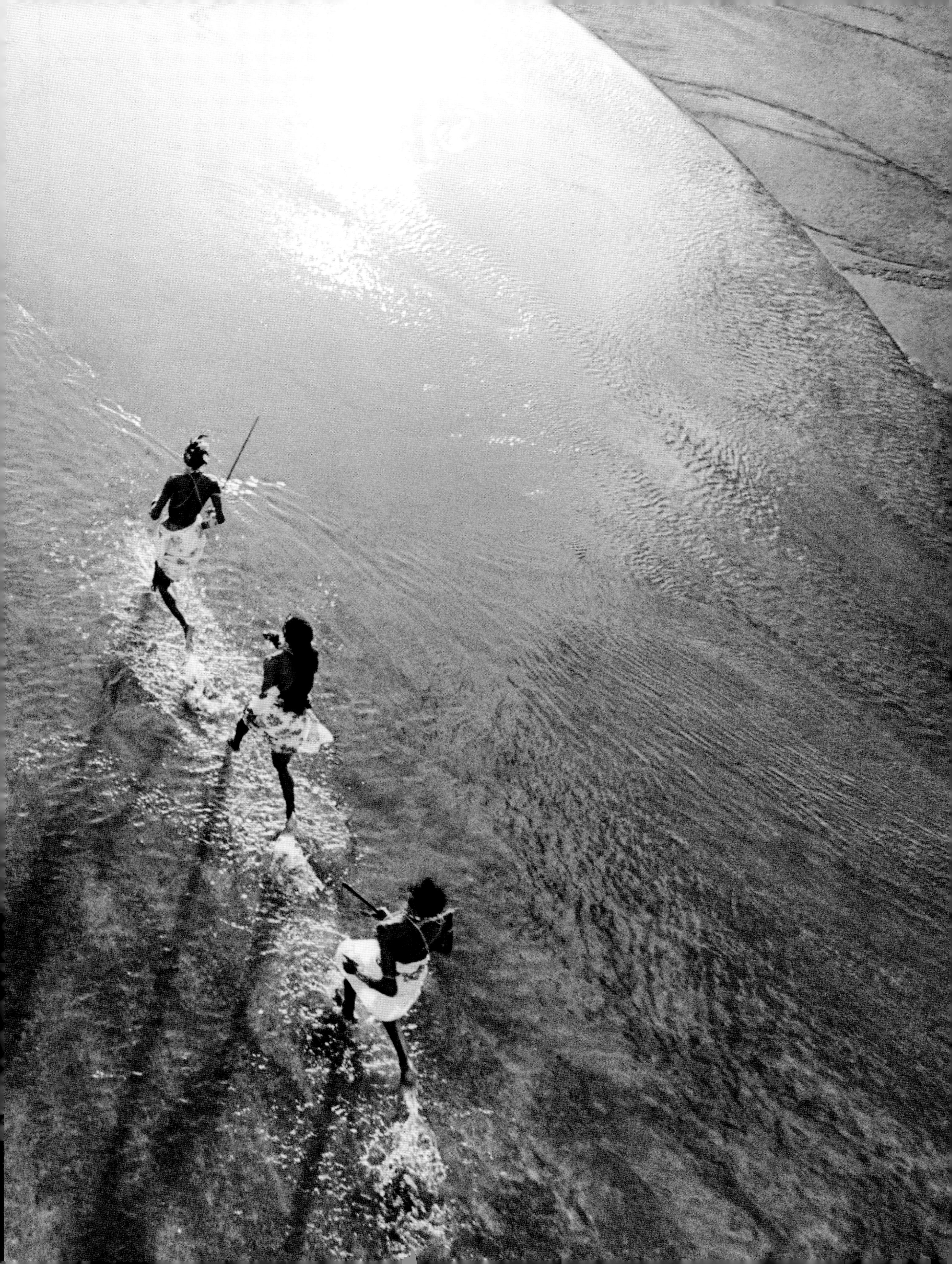

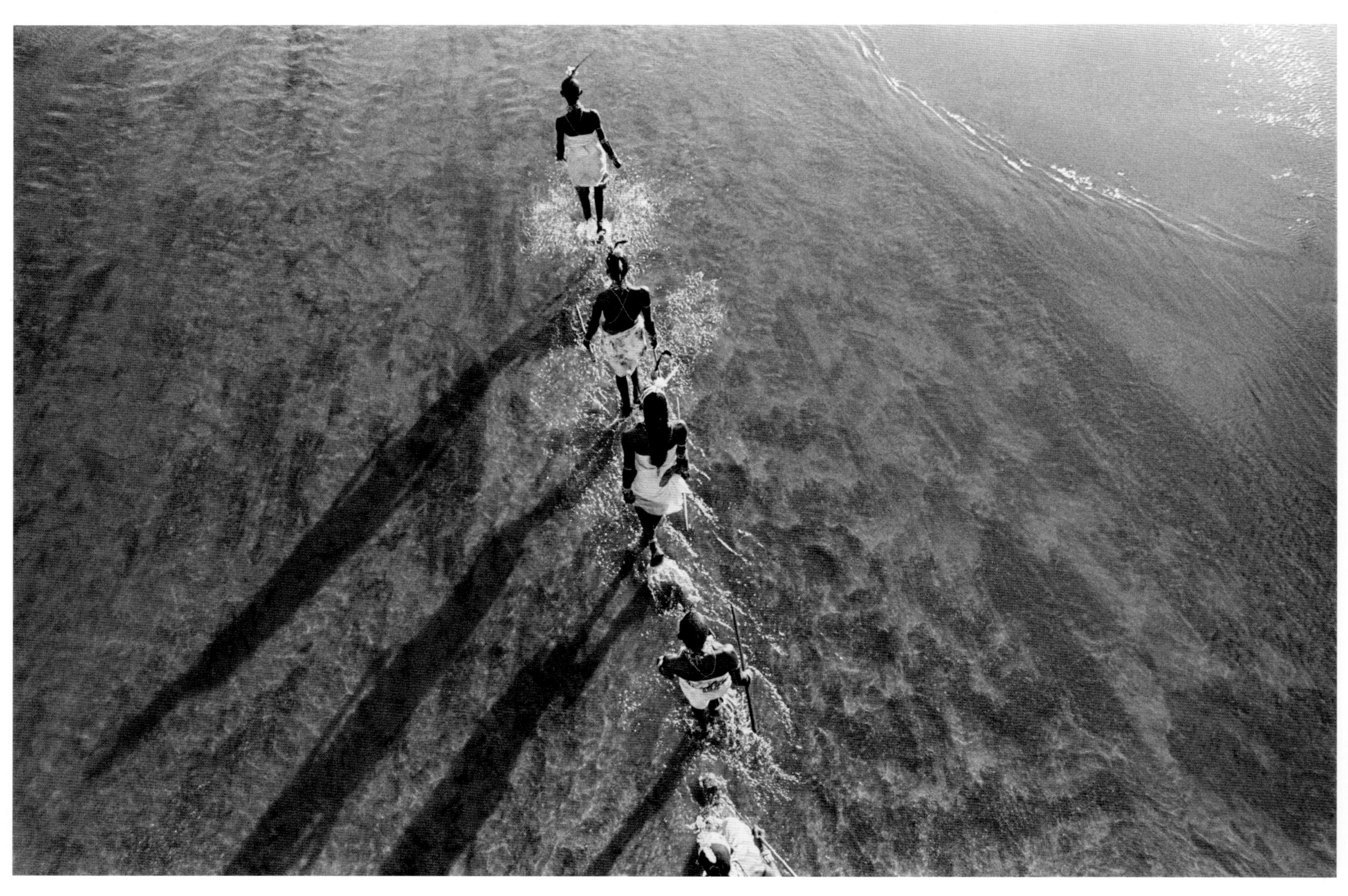

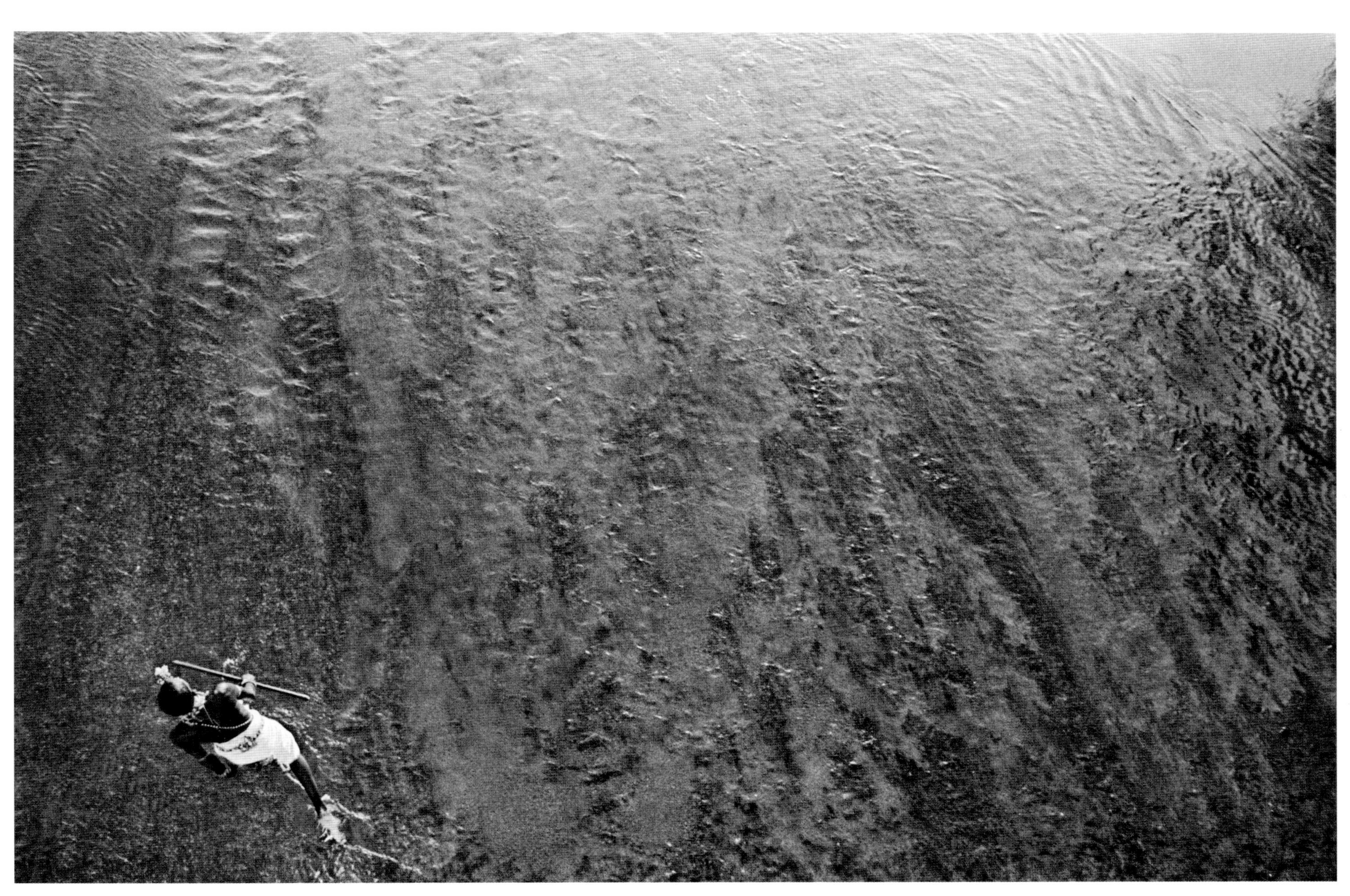

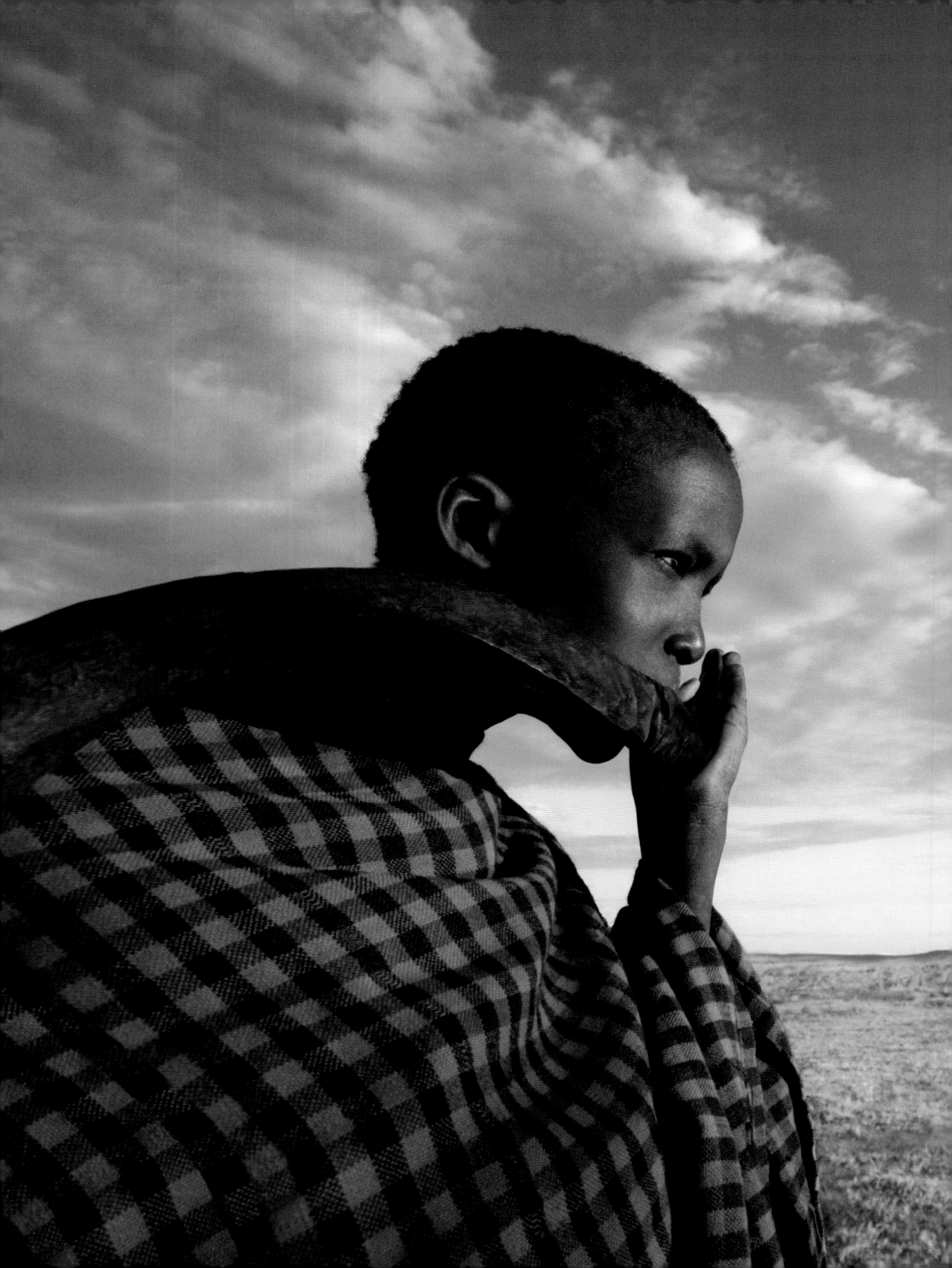

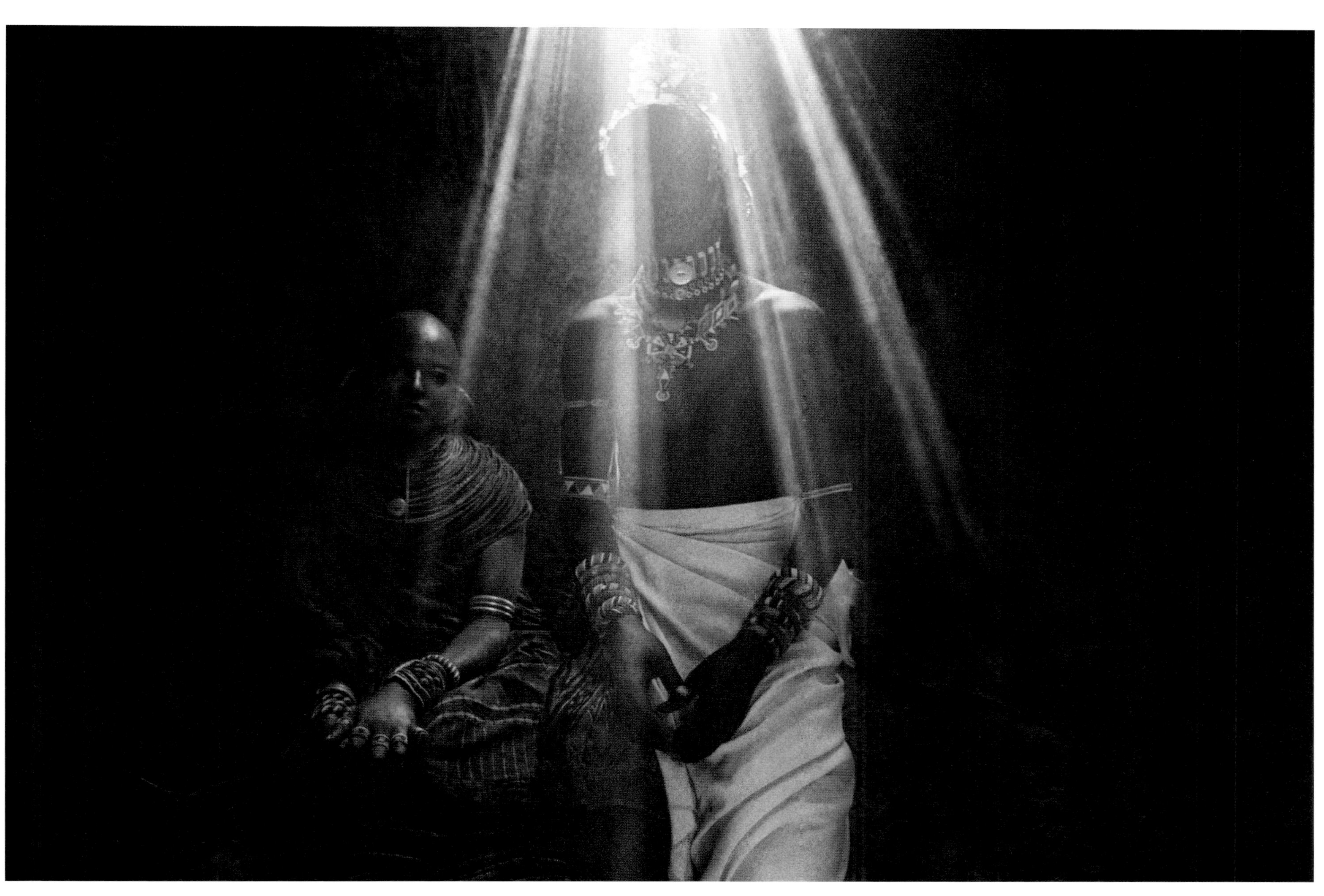

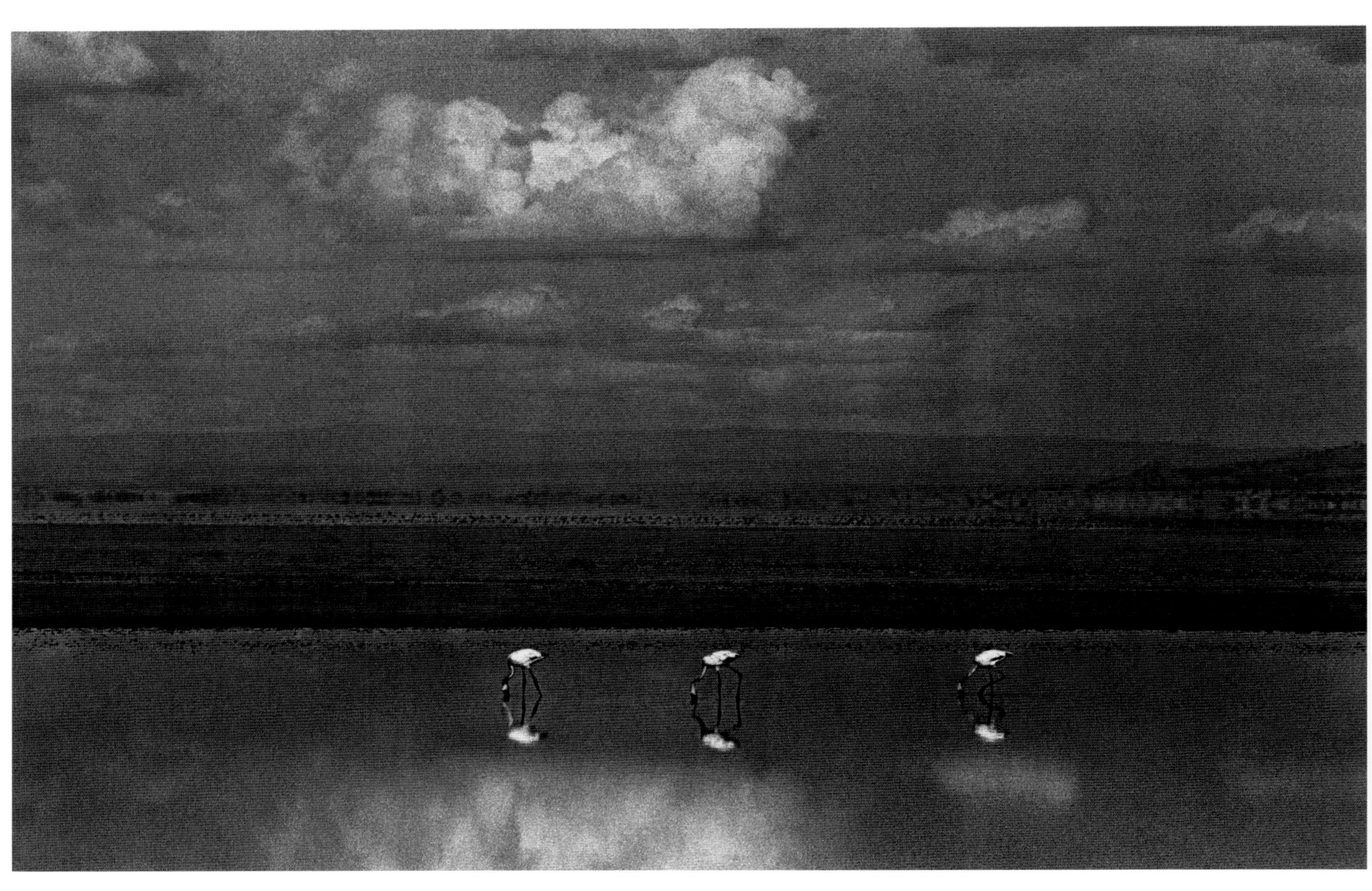

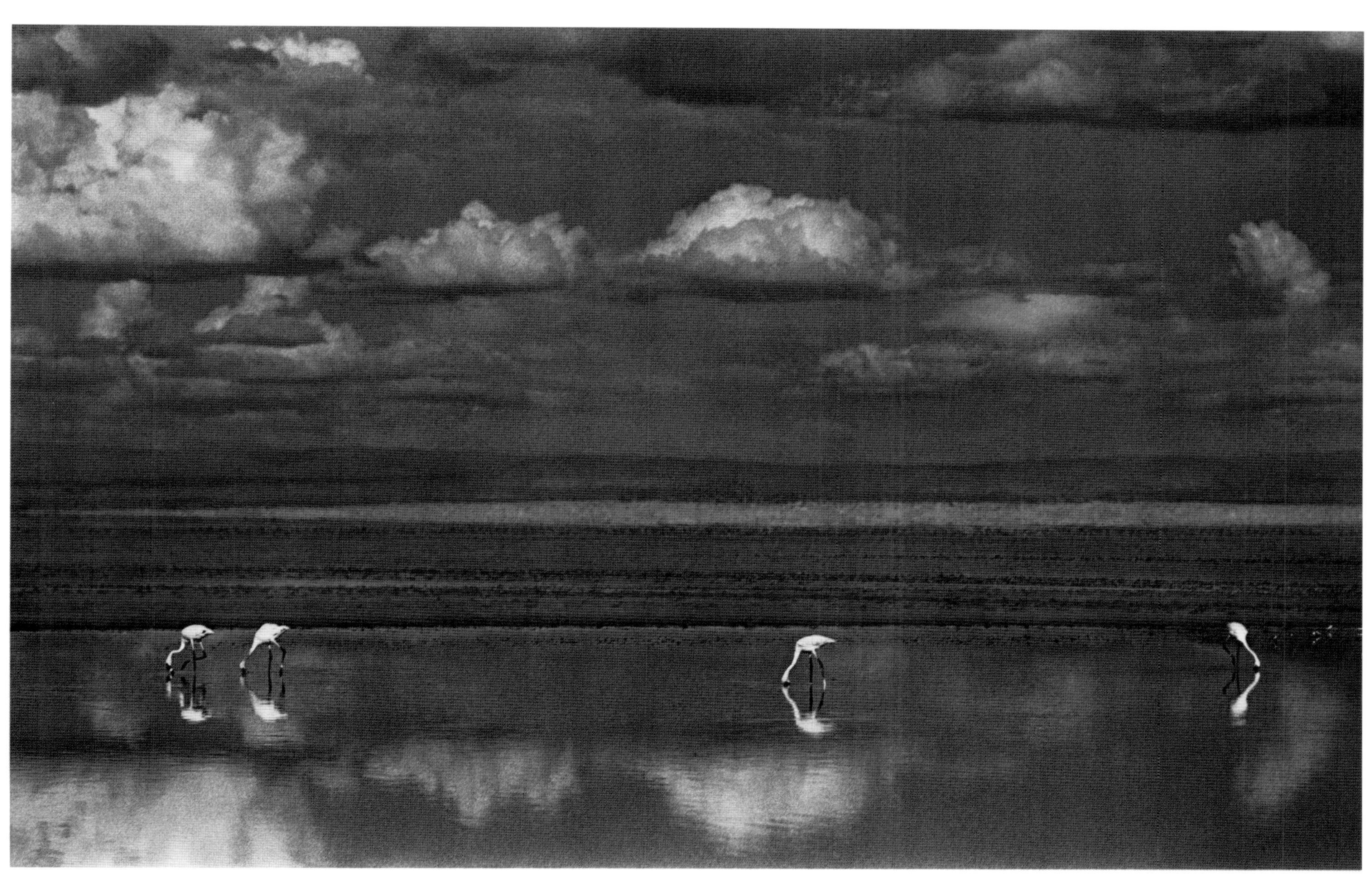

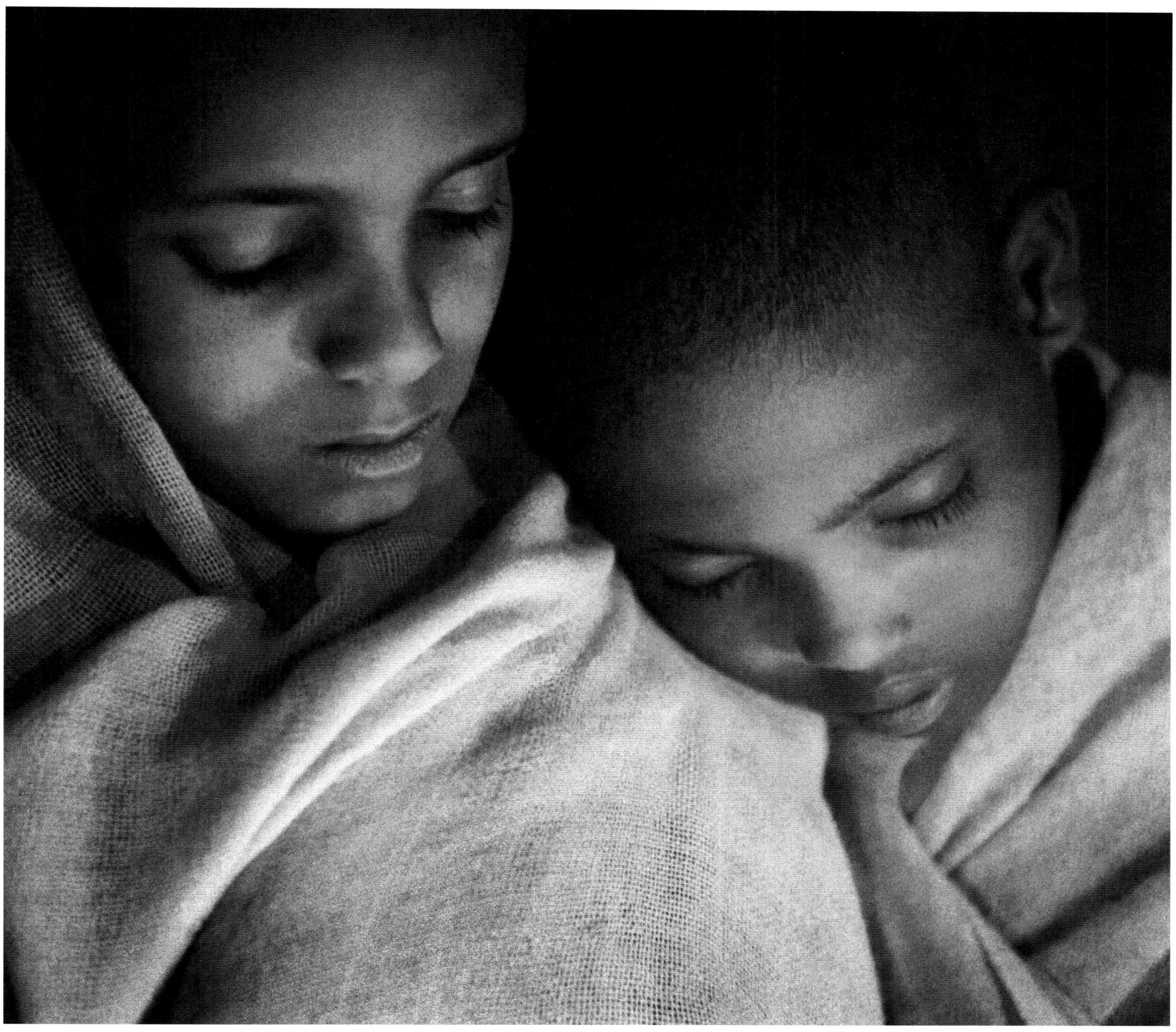

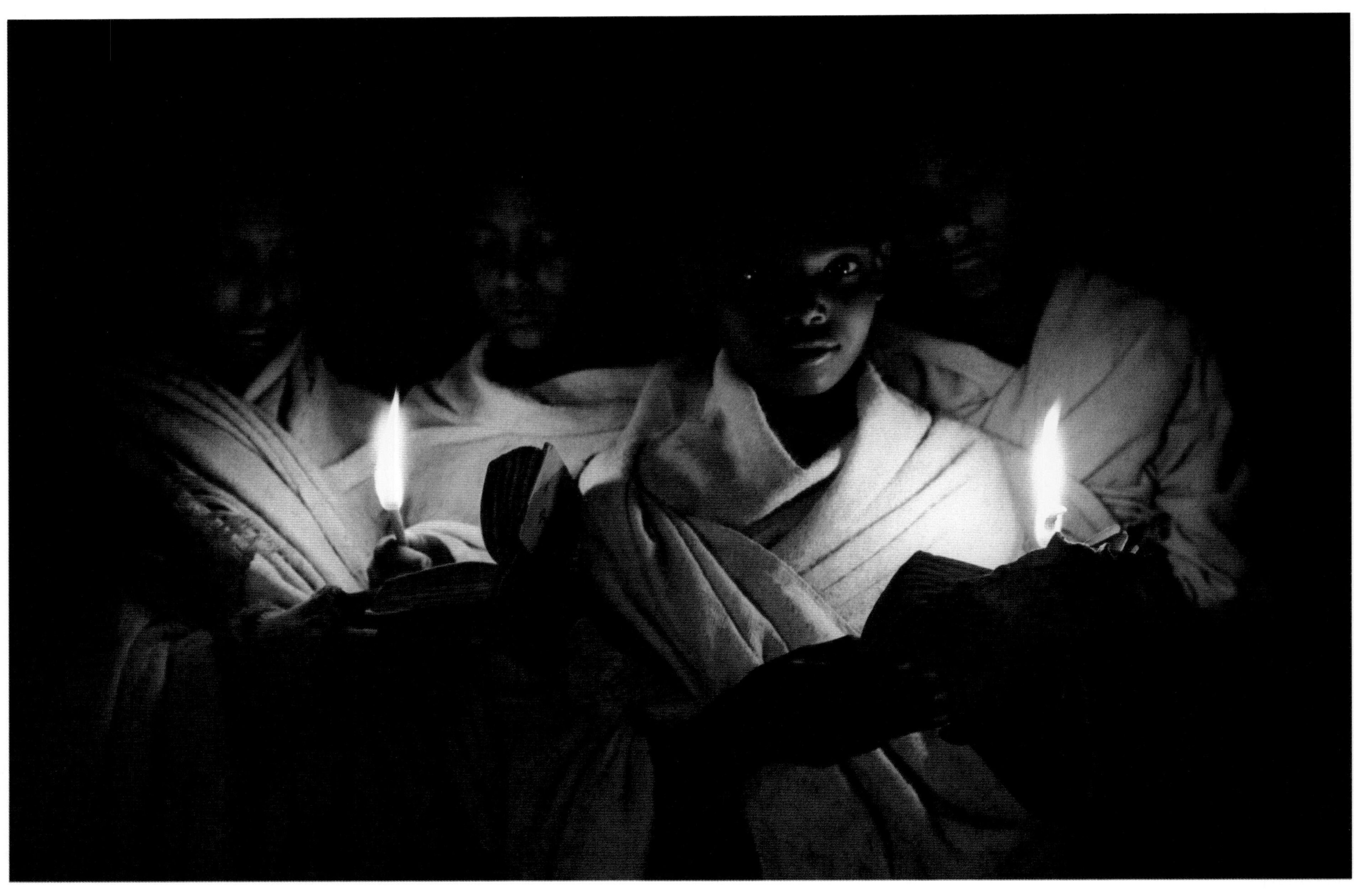

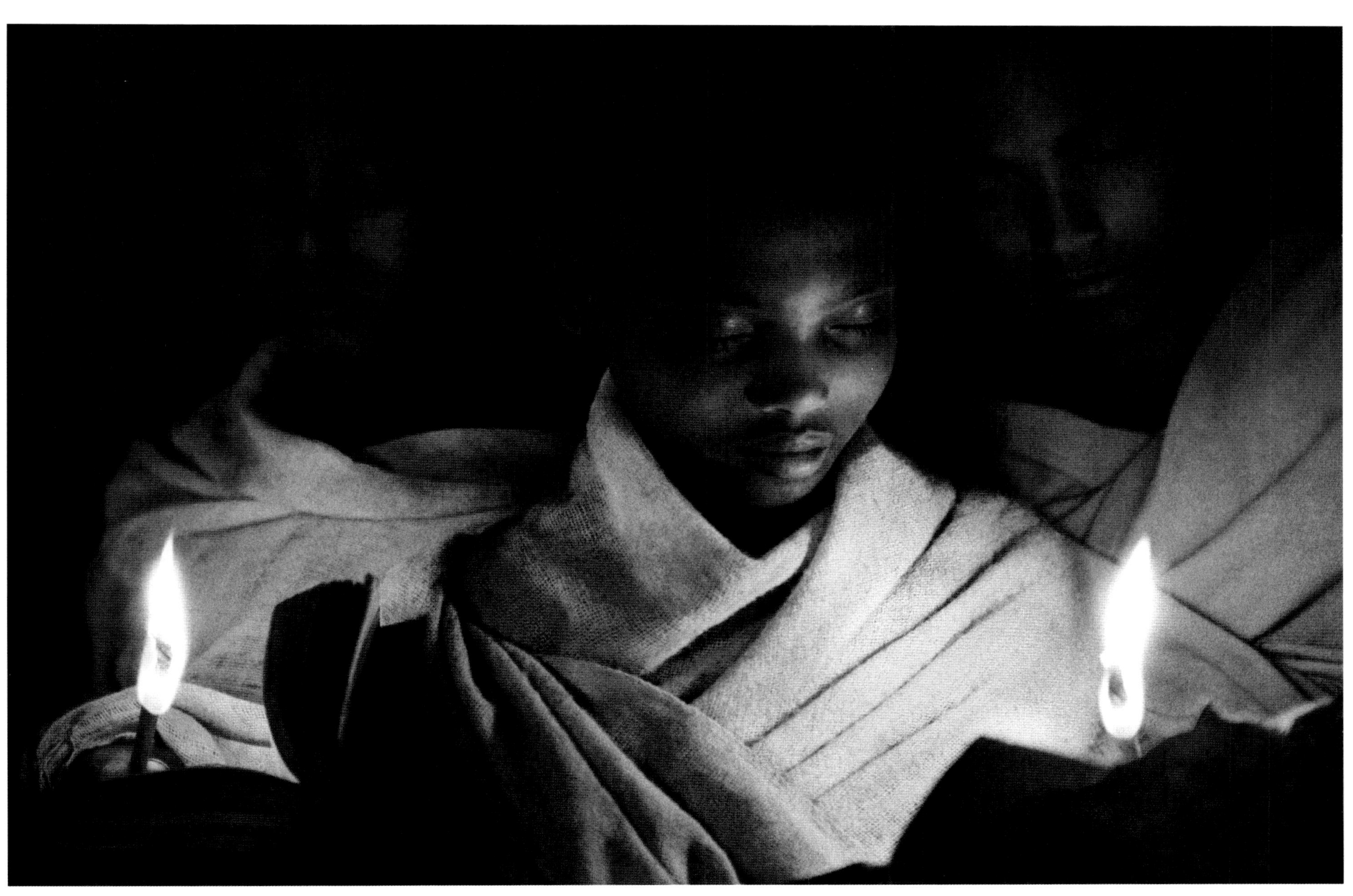

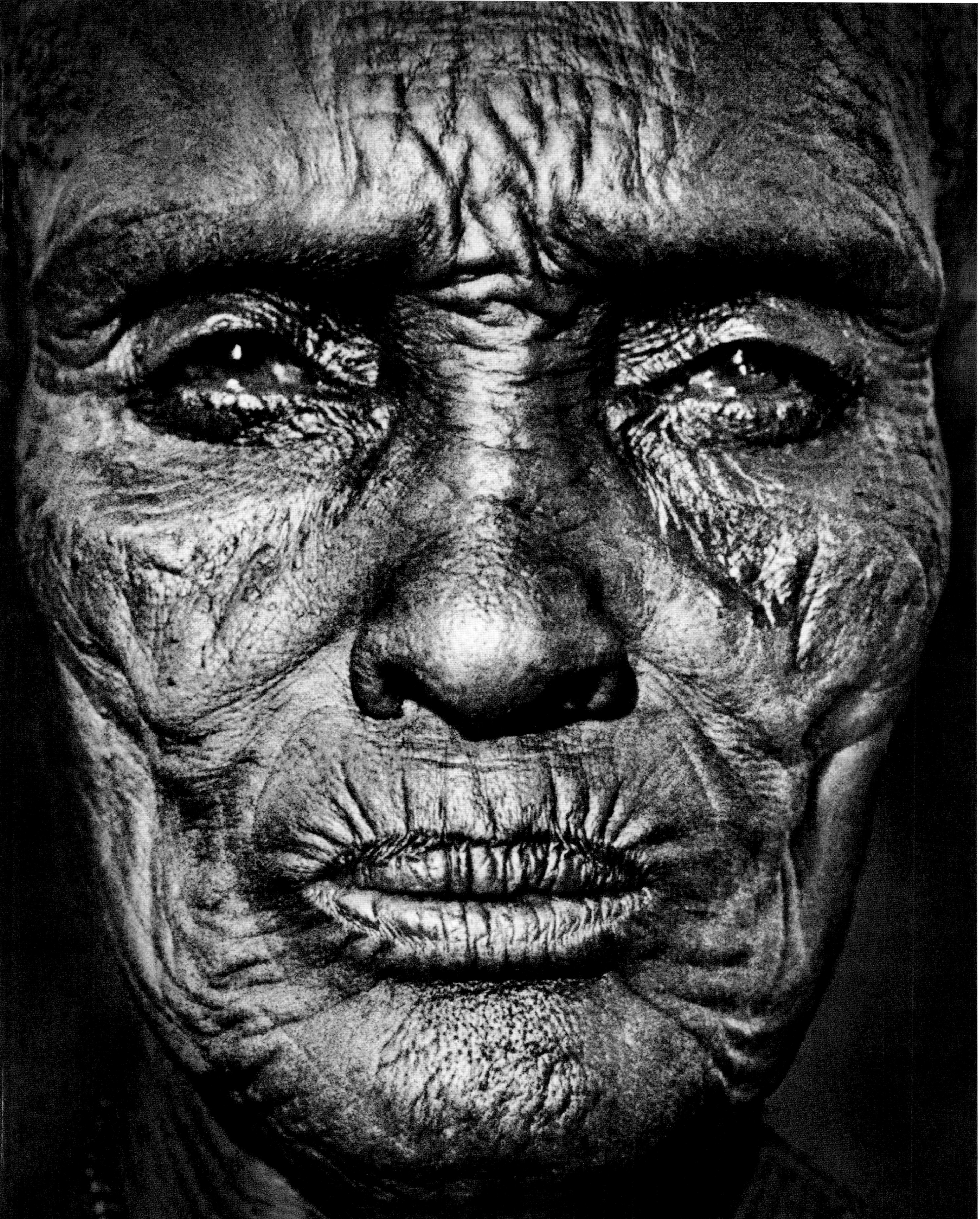

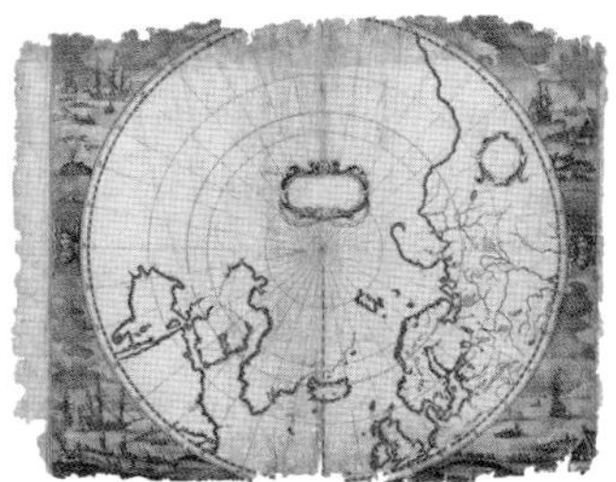

The Ancient Map

2006

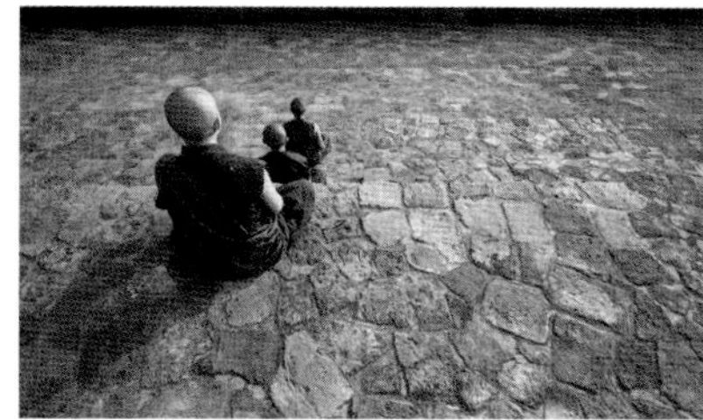

Totem

Nalanda, India
2001

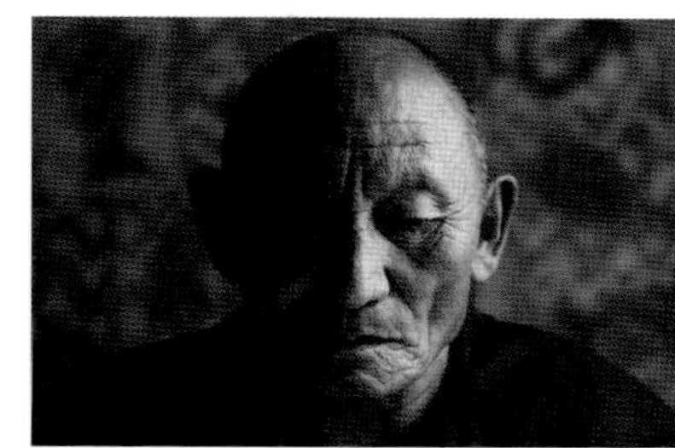

Palden

Daramsala, India
2001

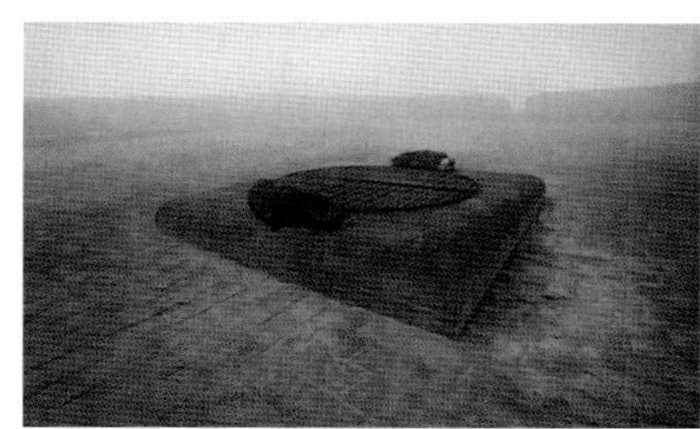

Nalanda Dream

Nalanda, India
2001

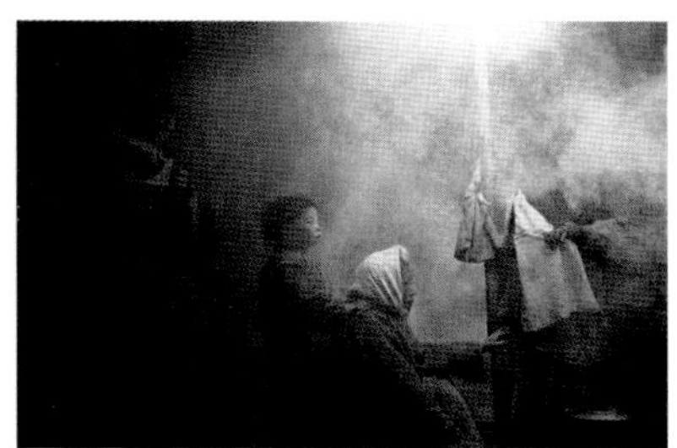

Nomads

Central Tibet
2002

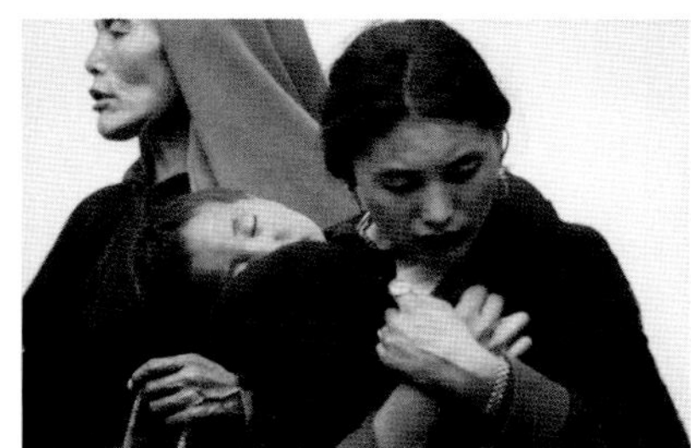

The Three Generations of Women

Tibet
2002

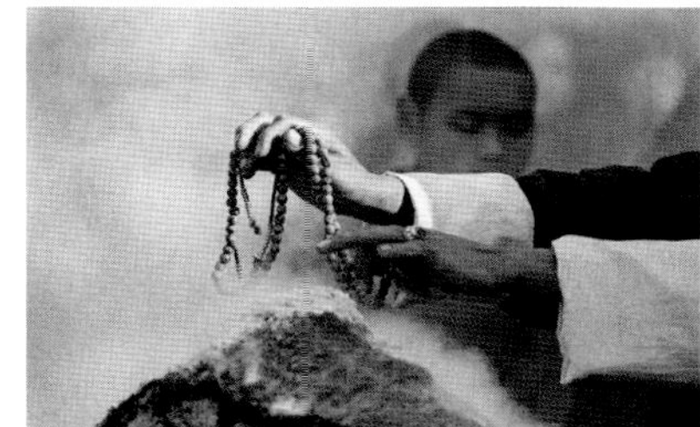

Mala

Tibet
2002

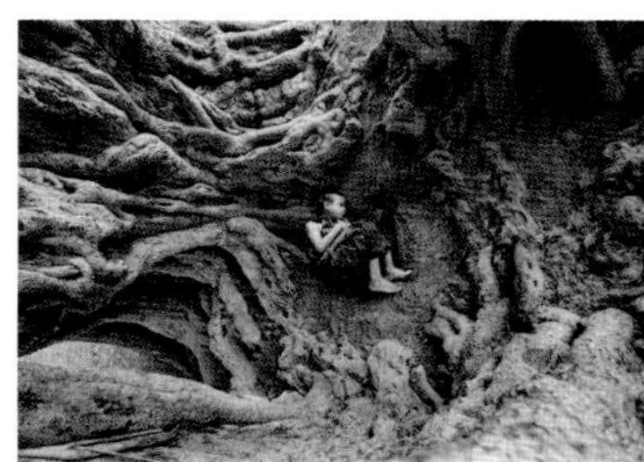

The Buddha Tree

Bodgaya, India
2001

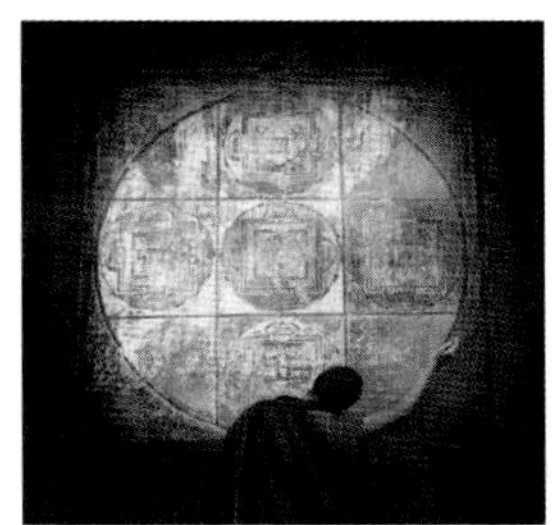

Mandala

Tibet
2002

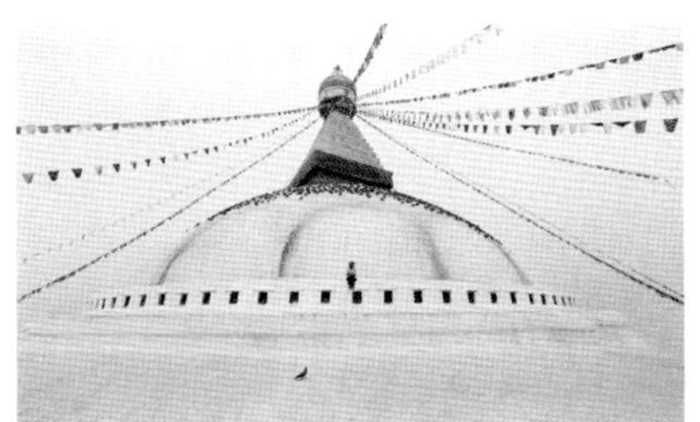

The Stupa and the Bird

Nepal
2001

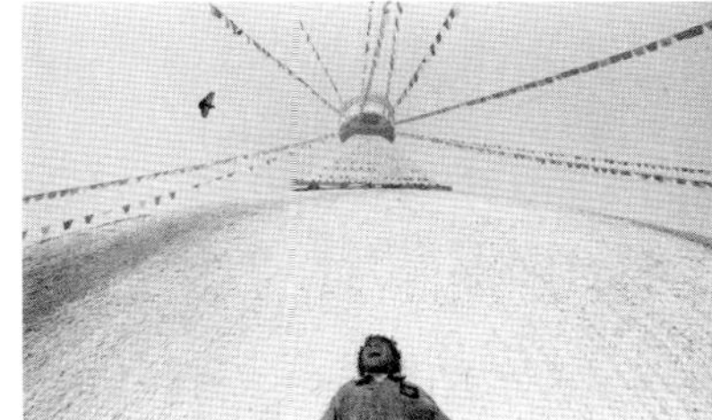

The Call

Nepal
2001

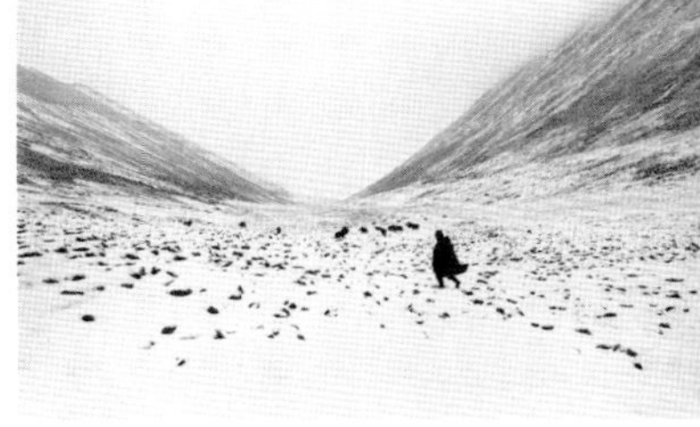

Passage

Tibet
2002

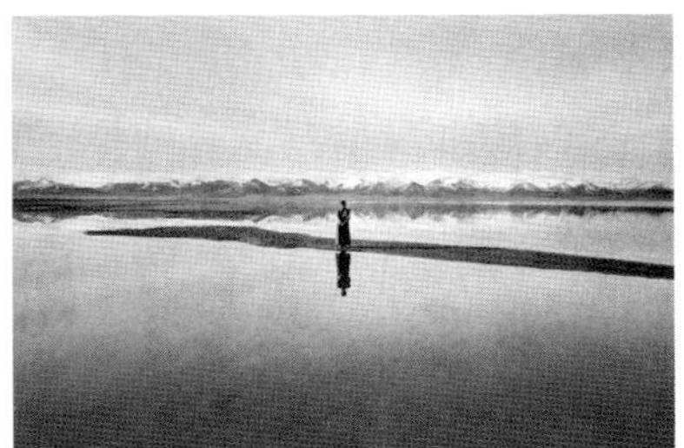

Namso

Tibet
2002

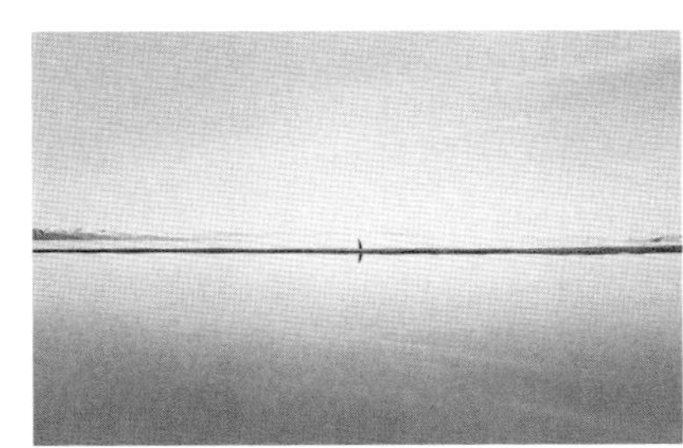

The Middle Path

Tibet
2002

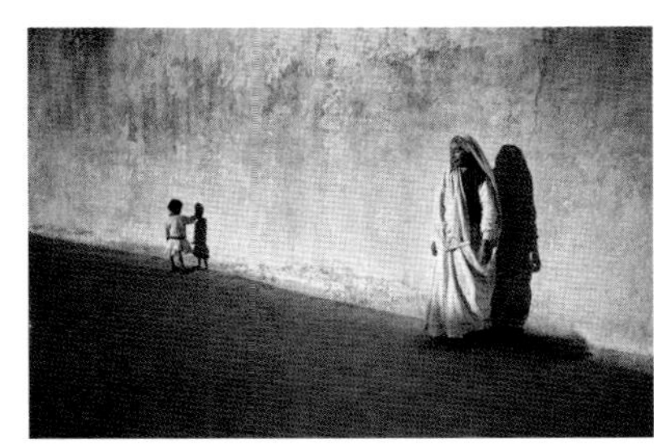

The Grandmother and the Child

Women's Jail, Jaipur, India
2000

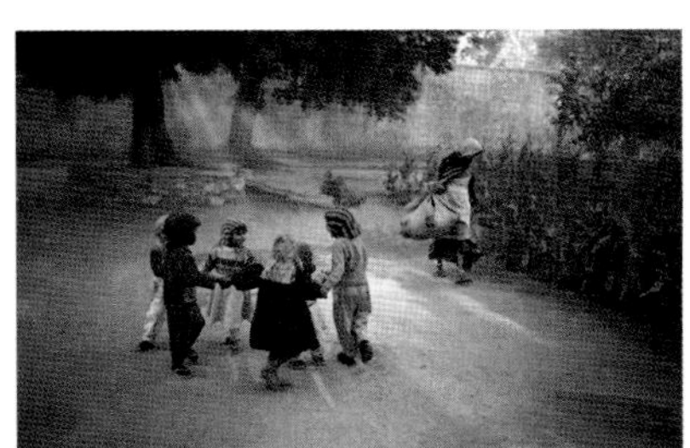

The Jail Game

India
2000

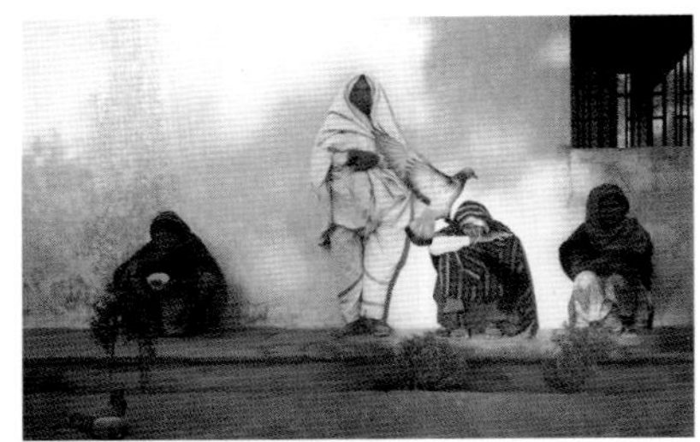

The Women and the Bird
India
2000

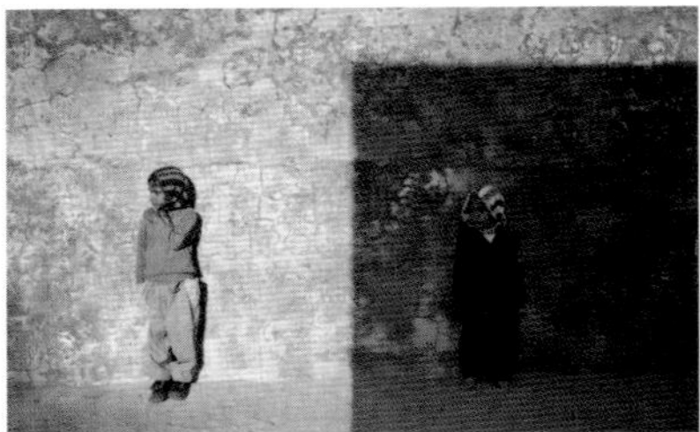

Light and Shadow
India
2000

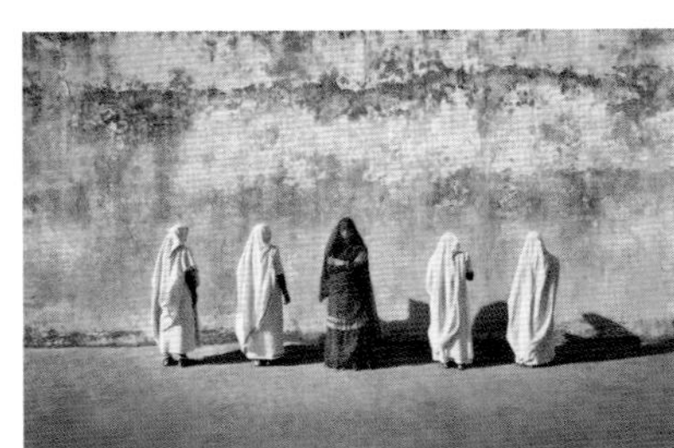

The Five Women
India
2000

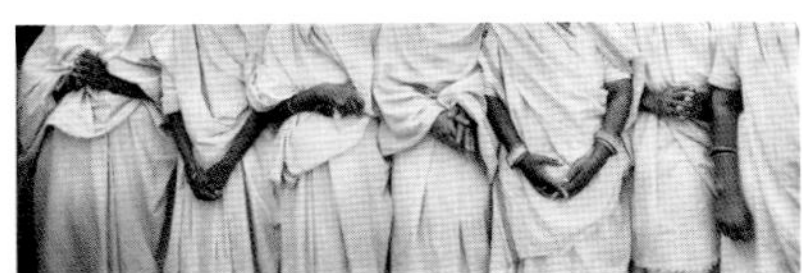

The Hands
India
2000

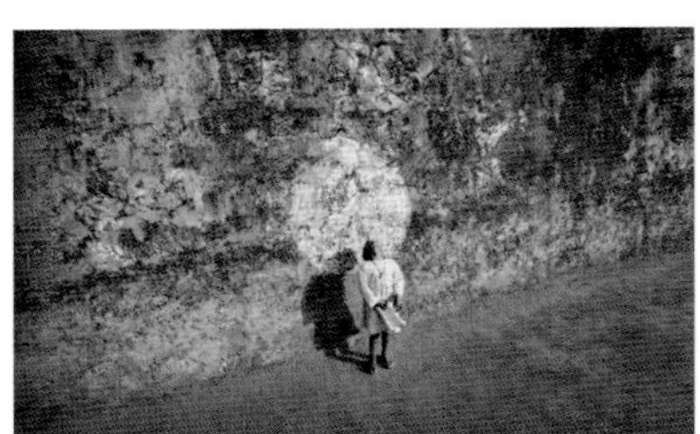

The Dance of the Sun
India
2000

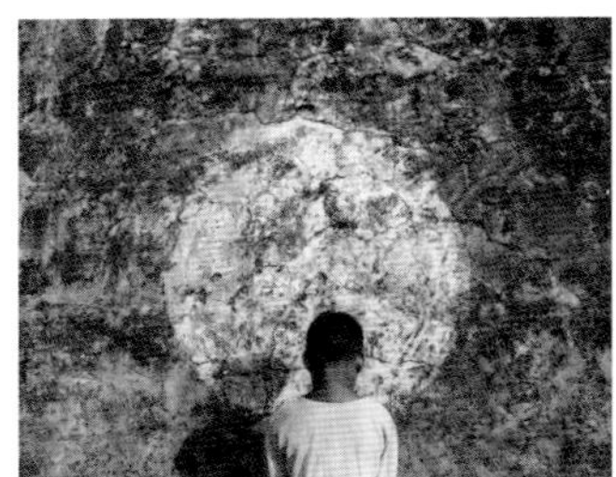

Sun
India
2000

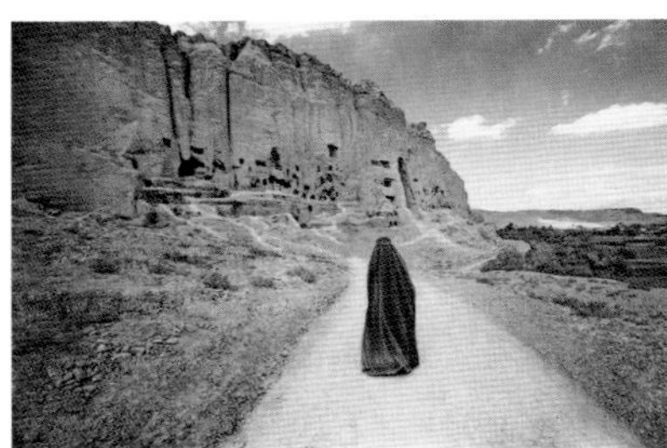

The Princess of Bamiyan
Afghanistan
2003

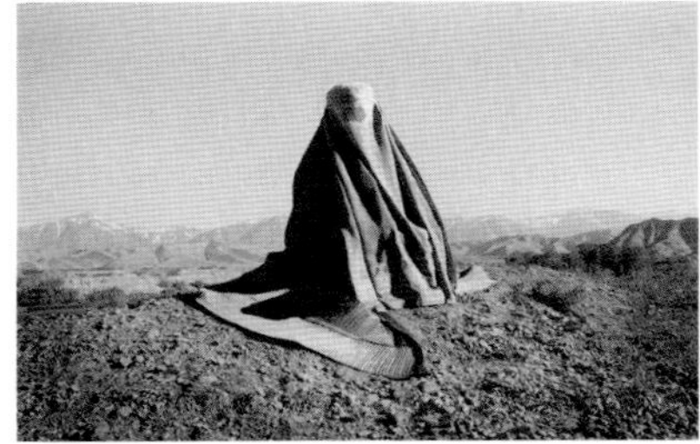

The Woman Mountain
Afghanistan
2003

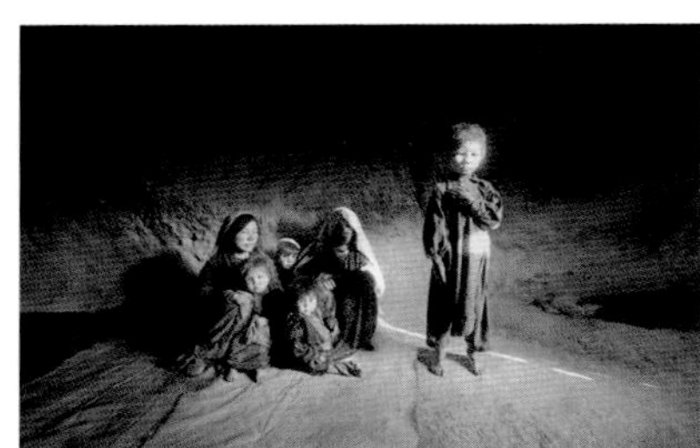

The Troglodyte Family
Afghanistan
2003

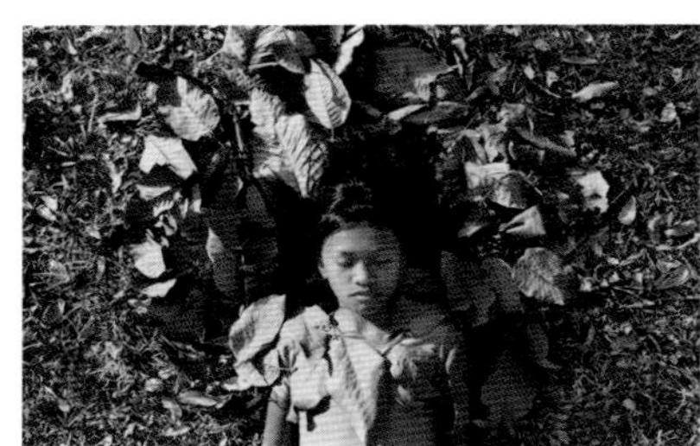

The Girl and the Dream Flower
Cambodia
2003

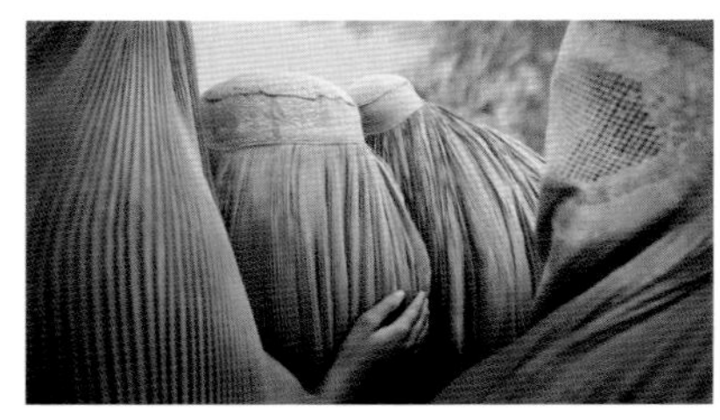

The Burka and the Hand
Afghanistan
2003

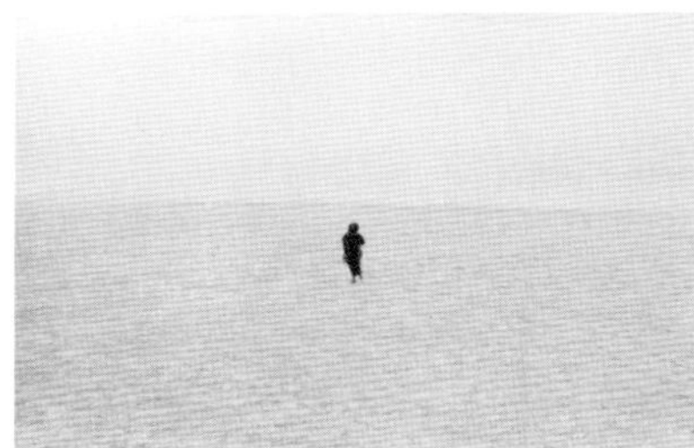

The Girl and Her Donkey I
Afghanistan
2003

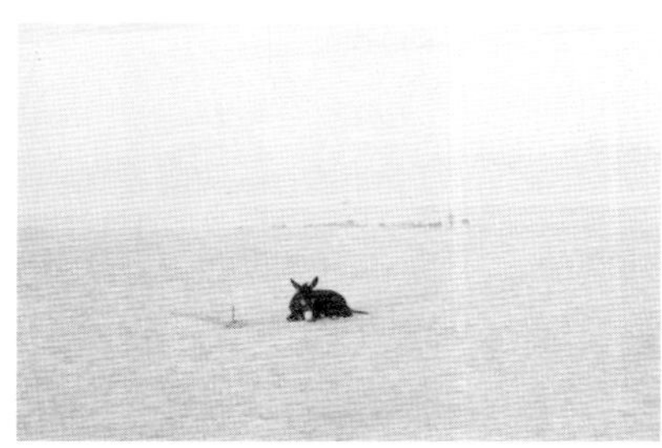

The Girl and Her Donkey II
Afghanistan
2003

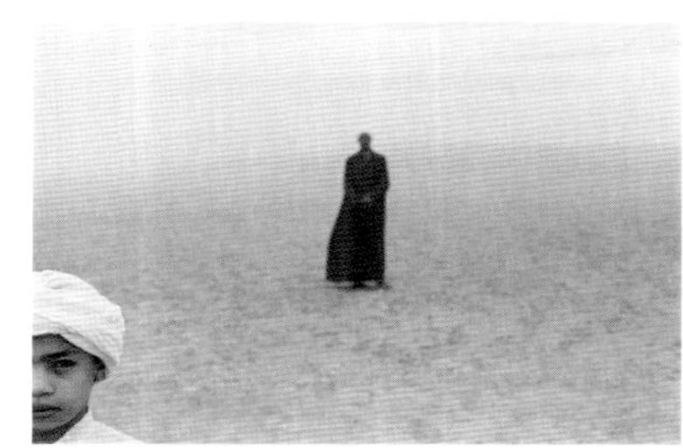

The Father
Egypt
2003

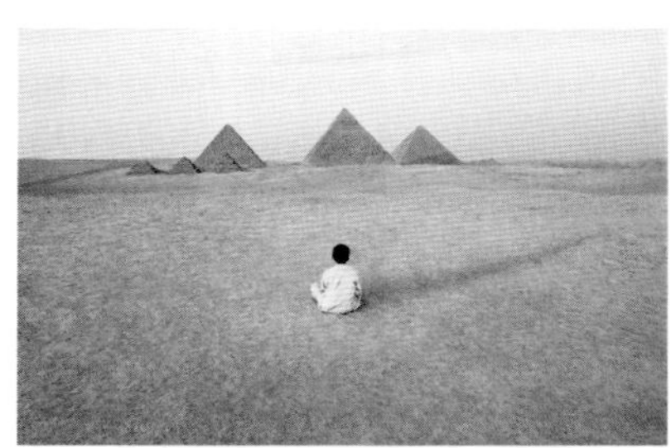

The Fourth Pyramid
Egypt
2003

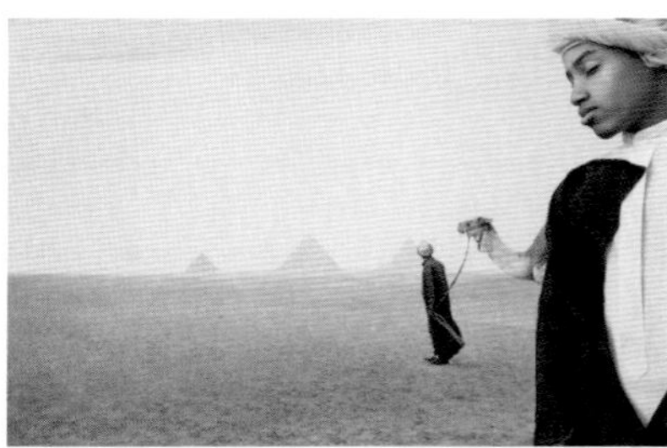

Memory
Egypt
2003

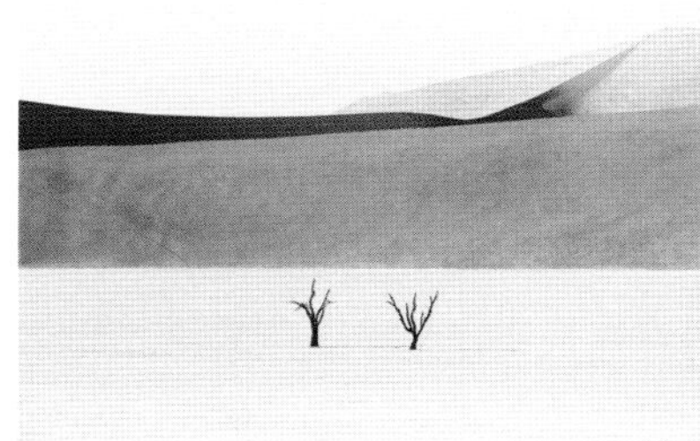

The Oldest Desert
Namibia
2004

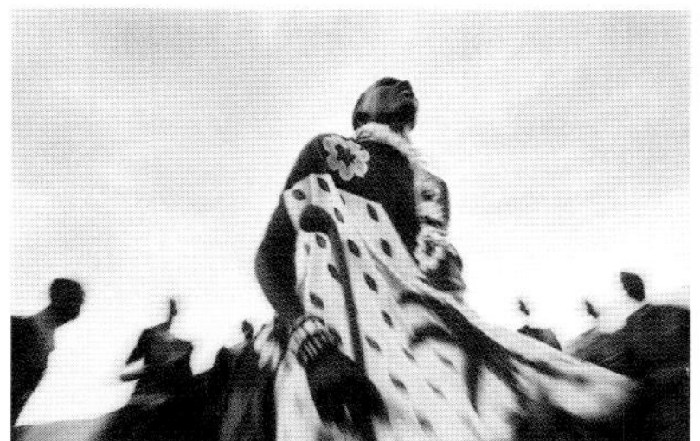

The Dance of the Rain
Kenya
2004

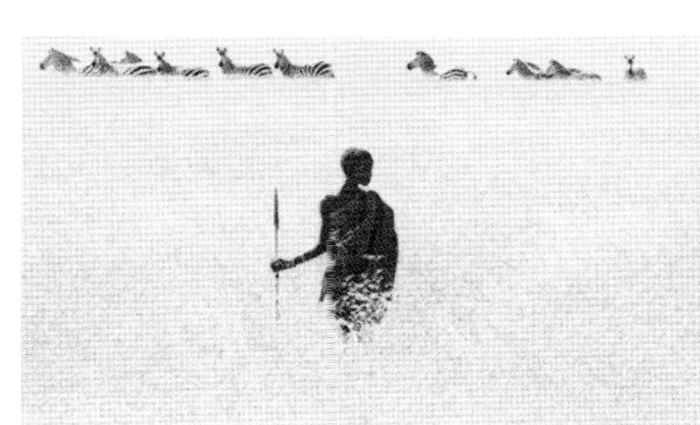

The Zebra's Keeper
Kenya
2004

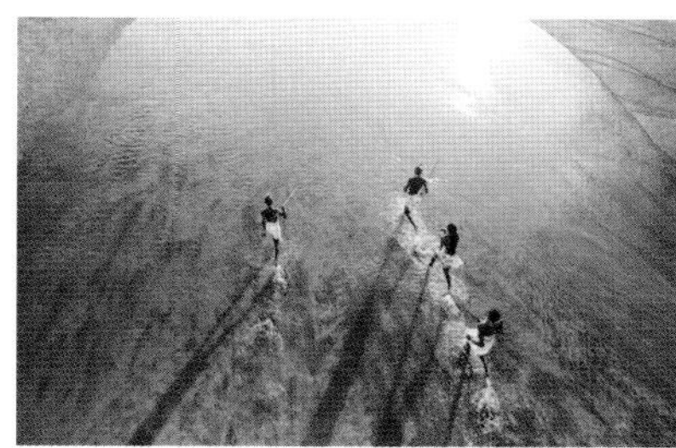

The Run I
Kenya
2004

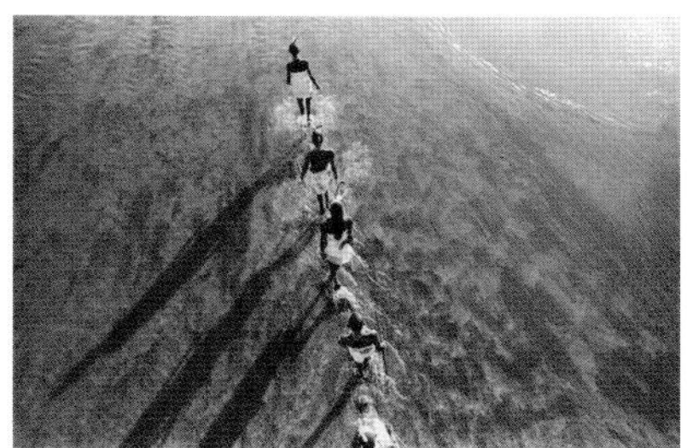

The Run II
Kenya
2004

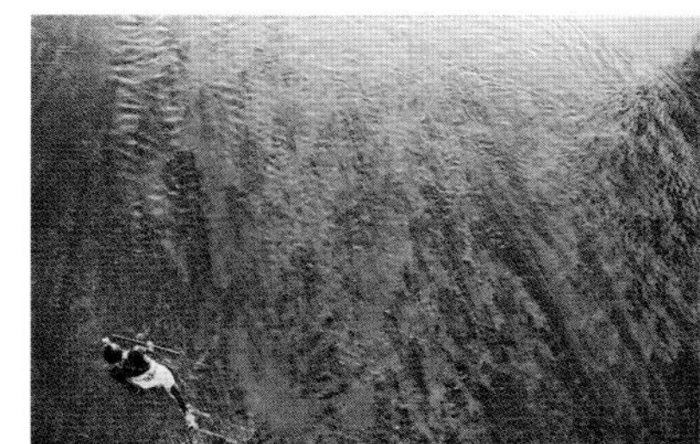

The Run III
Kenya
2004

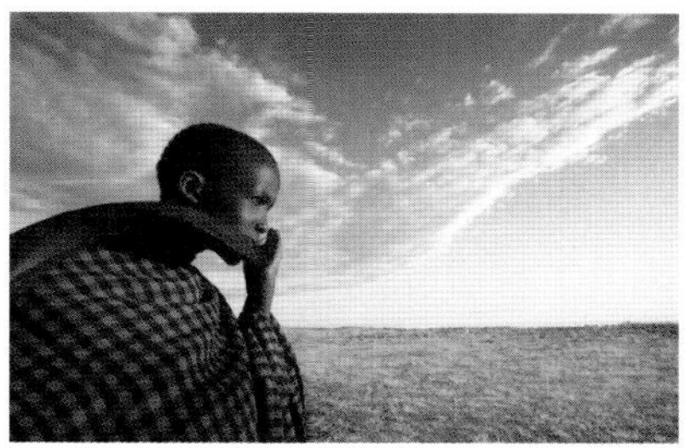

The Whispers of the Clouds
Kenya
2004

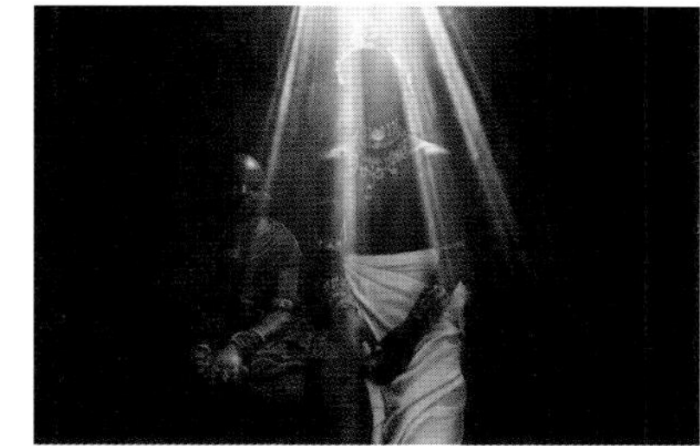

The New Married
Kenya
2004

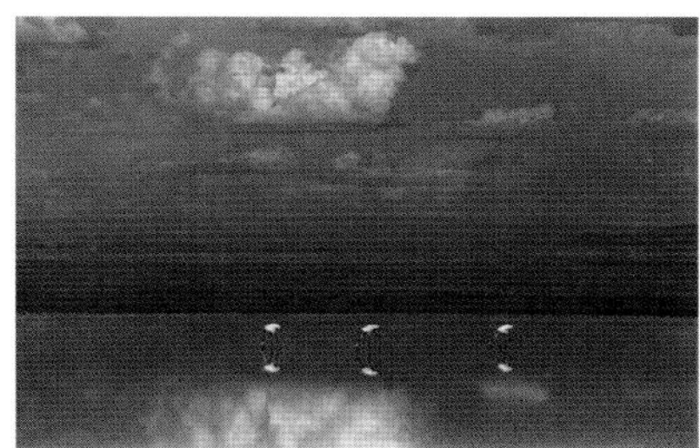

The White Birds Coming from the Sky I
Kenya
2004

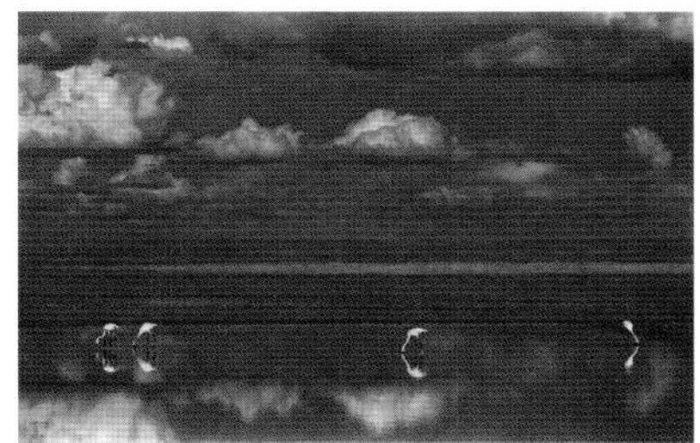

The White Birds Coming from the Sky II
Kenya
2004

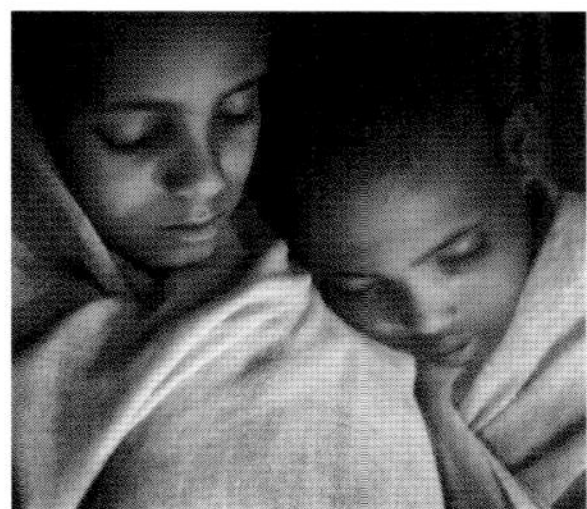

The Angels
Ethiopia
2006

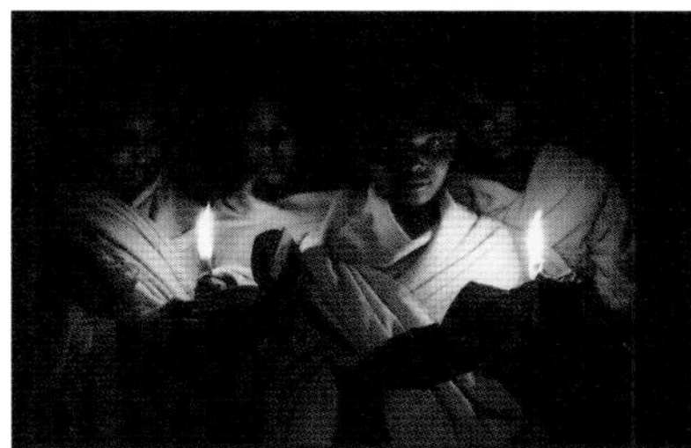

The Disappeared Children
Ethiopia
2006

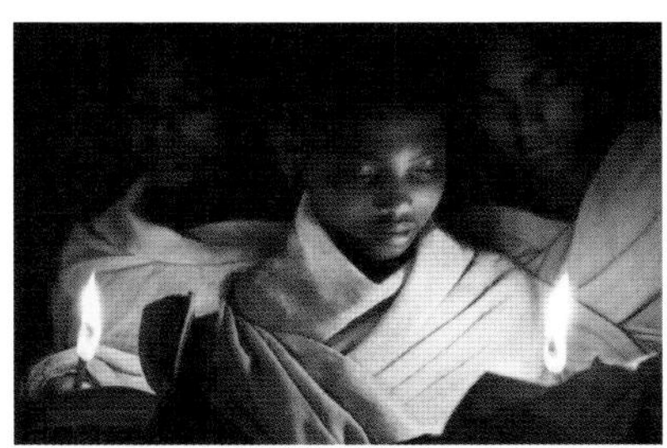

Trinity
Ethiopia
2006

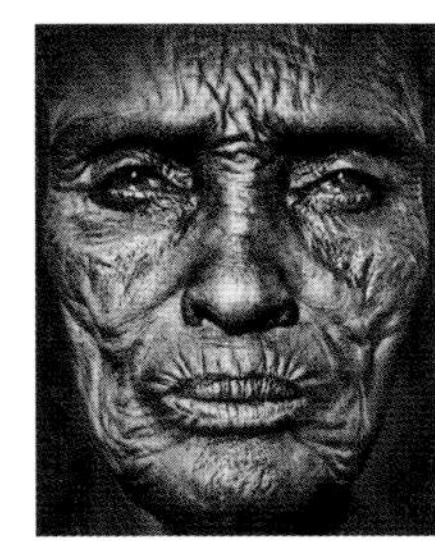

The Old Lady
Kenya
2004

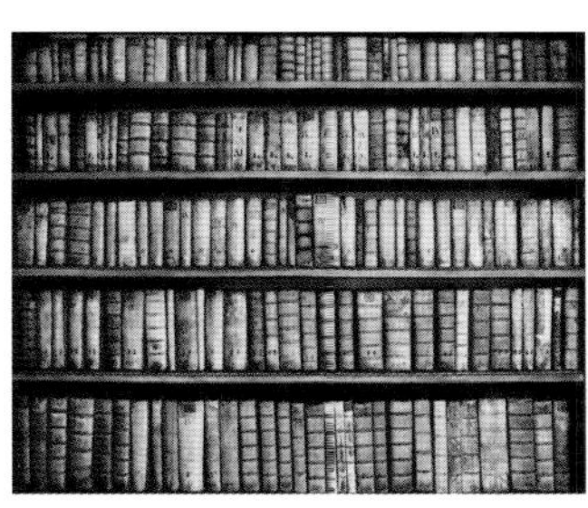

Library of Knowledge
Prague
2007

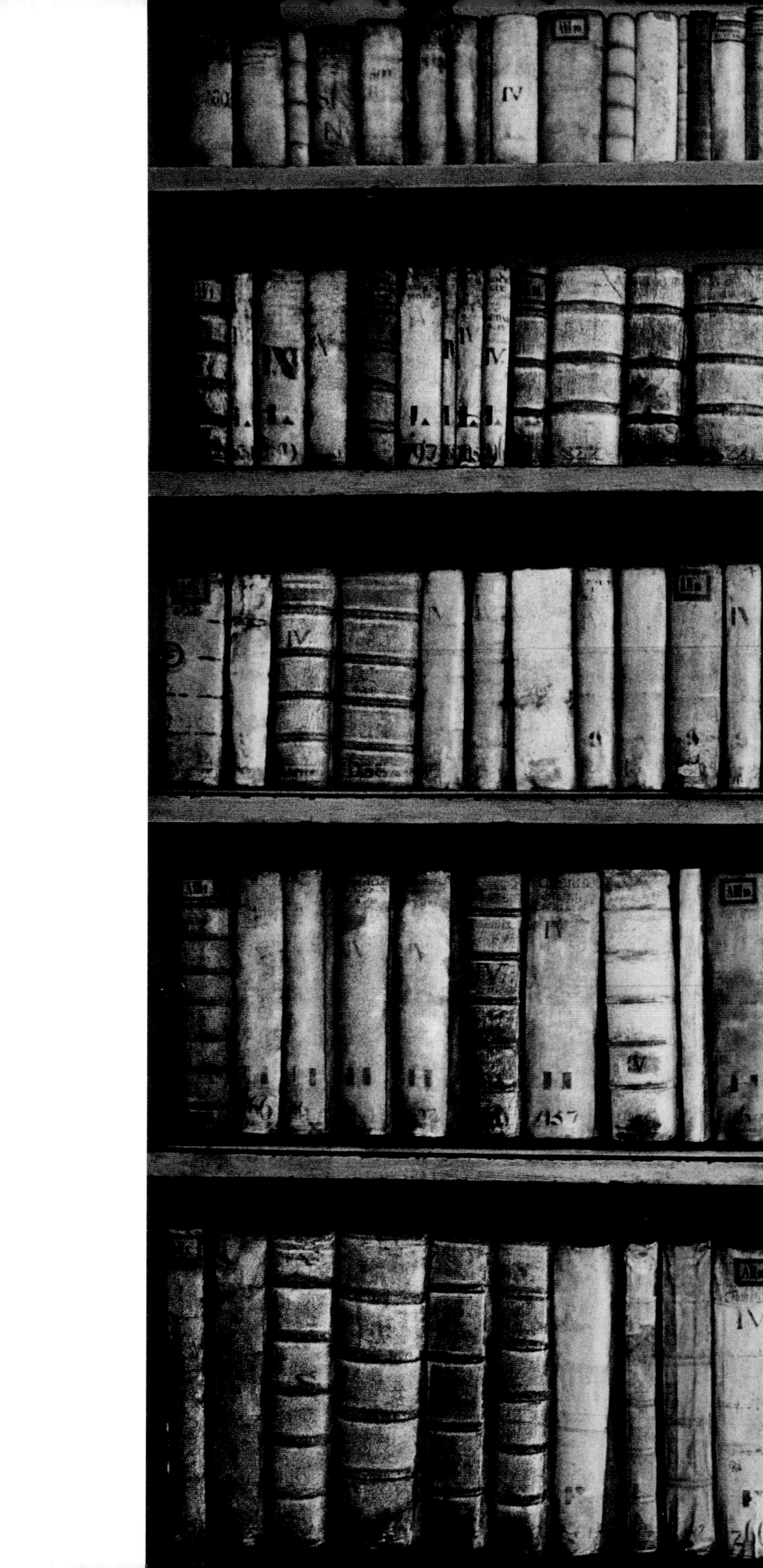

Through her photographs, Caroline Halley des Fontaines shows us a world in which the evocation of Self and Other is an endeavour that fully reaffirms the place of humanity.

One by one, as the multiple facets of this universe reveal themselves, the images speak to us. They describe a history that ignores national boundaries from one end of the globe to the other, with no apparent links to a specific culture that might distinguish one image from another. The depth of the image does not lie in the soil from which it sprang. Environments evoke the roads humans have wandered only to settle down one day either by choice or by involuntary restraint.

These images have a thousand faces, yet one can affirm that they are but a single face—the face of humanity ravaged by a thousand years of history, reduced to a silhouette, a glance, a dazzling gesture captured by the eye of the photographer. It is a silhouette that speaks of the ceaseless movement by which humans continue to create themselves. Before this single face of Man, time unrolls, establishing itself in the silence. "Time and Silence," it tells us. With this title alone, announcing an intimate experience, we are invited to traverse time and leave behind us the fantasies of modern societies so tied up in their conquests, their technologies and their desires born out of a life of leisure.

These photographs create the experience of loss and of a slipping toward other territories. With subtlety, the artist opens up the poetic, spiritual and political elements that constitute, figuratively, the world in which she wanders, from body to body, in touch with a transitory reality.

By this very strong involvement with her subject, the artist invites us to take stock of an ancestral loss and to discover the vibrant signs that dwell at the center of societies in permanent struggle for their futures. To become, or rather *go toward* somewhere else that holds safe that element in each person that is the essence of being human. An elsewhere in an in-between place where lies the burden of the everyday and an imaginary limned in timelessness that is captured in images of women in the prisons of India, Tibetans in their places of exile, Saharan desert nomads in a place of memory, Afghan Hazaras wherever they take refuge, and Tanzanian Masais enduring their rituals.

Henceforth, we create a mental image of the road still to be traveled so that we no longer have to resort to the ordinary in speaking of Self as *I*; we live it as an experience of Self as *We*. The image is thus at once a place of construction and a place of loss. It is attached to a world that can only see it through the prism of its physical settings. The Real appears here revealing itself little by little through clouds of fog, in the halos of the light that pierce the darkness. It is revealed in the elegance of the aesthete who loses herself in ephemeral contemplation, in the respectful accompaniment of its subject colored by a distancing from which emerge the mysteries that the photographer intends to preserve. Time multiplies itself infinitely, and spaces pile one on top of another.

These photographs by Caroline Halley des Fontaines invite us to a universe where the narrowing down of experience, captured in all its fragility, is what creates its narrative structure. A world—a history—where the image is only the mark left by the experience, musical as well as silent, the better to grasp the fault lines of the Real.

Alexandra Baudelot
Art critic and author

In ihren Fotos zeigt uns Caroline Halley des Fontaines eine Welt, in der uns die Begegnung zwischen dem Selbst und dem Anderen den Ort des Menschen ins Bewusstsein ruft.

Nach und nach offenbaren sich die zahlreichen Facetten dieser Welt, und die Bilder sprechen zu uns. Sie erzählen eine Geschichte, die Länder rund um den Globus umschließt, ohne auf Grenzen Rücksicht zu nehmen, ohne erkennbare Verbindung zu einer spezifischen Kultur, durch die sich die Bilder voneinander unterscheiden ließen. Die Intensität der Bilder rührt nicht von dem Ort ihres Ursprungs her, der nur das Umfeld der Wege ist, die der Mensch zurücklegen musste, um eines Tages stehen zu bleiben – manchmal aus eigenem Antrieb, manchmal durch unfreiwillige Abhängigkeiten.

Diese Bilder haben tausend Gesichter, und dennoch können wir von ihnen behaupten, sie hätten nur ein einziges – das einer Menschheit, die eine jahrtausendealte Geschichte durchlebt hat, die sich in einer Silhouette, einem Blick, einer Geste widerspiegelt. Die das Auge der Fotografin eingefangen hat und uns von der unablässigen Bewegung erzählt, mit der die Menschen sich beständig neu erschaffen. Vor diesem Gesicht zieht eine Zeit vorbei, die sich in der Stille behauptet: „Time and Silence". Mit diesem schlichten Titel, der eine intime Erfahrung ankündigt, werden wir eingeladen, durch die Zeit zu reisen und die Trugbilder der modernen Zivilisation hinter uns zu lassen, die mit den Errungenschaften, Technologien und Wünschen des Freizeitlebens verbunden sind.

Unser Blick macht hier die Erfahrung des Verlustes und des Hinübergleitens in andere Regionen. Die Künstlerin zeigt uns mit kleinen Gesten die poetischen, spirituellen und politischen Elemente, die im bildlichen Sinne die Welt ausmachen, durch die sie wandelt, von Nahem und in direktem Kontakt mit einer vergänglichen Wirklichkeit.

Vollständig eingenommen von ihrem Thema, lädt sie uns ein, uns auf neue Erfahrungen einzulassen und die lebendigen Zeichen im Herzen der Gesellschaft zu erkennen, die sich in einem permanenten Kampf um ihr Werden befindet. Werden – das bedeutet Entwicklung hin zu etwas Anderem, zu einem Anderswo, um den Wesenskern der Menschheit zu erhalten, der jedem innewohnt. Ein Anderswo, angesiedelt in dem Raum zwischen der Last des täglichen Lebens und der Imagination der Zeitlosigkeit, den das Bild einfängt. Das kann das Bild von Frauen in den Gefängnissen Indiens sein, von Tibetern in ihrem Exil, von Tuaregs an einem Ort des Gedenkens, von Hazaras in ihrer Zuflucht oder von Massai bei ihren Ritualen.

Wir sehen den Weg vor uns, den wir noch zurücklegen müssen, damit wir in unserem täglichen Leben nicht mehr von uns selbst allein als *Ich* sprechen, sondern unser Selbst als *Wir* erfahren. Das Bild ist folglich zugleich ein Ort des Werdens und des Vergehens. Es ist mit einer Welt verbunden, die ausschließlich durch das Prisma ihrer Inszenierungen lesbar wird. Die Wirklichkeit erscheint, nachdem sie hinter Nebelschleiern sichtbar wird, in verschwommenen Lichtkreisen, welche die Dunkelheit durchdringen. Eleganz der Ästhetin, die sich der flüchtigen Kontemplation hingibt, und ihr respektvoll begleitetes Thema durch Verfremdung einfärbt, so dass Geheimnisse zum Vorschein kommen, welche die Fotografin gut zu hüten versteht. Die Zeit wird ins Unendliche multipliziert, und die Orte überlagern sich.

Caroline Halley des Fontaines' Fotos laden uns ein in eine Welt, deren Erzählstruktur durch reduzierte, in ihrer Zerbrechlichkeit gefangene Erfahrungen bestimmt wird. Eine Welt – eine Geschichte –, in der das Bild nicht mehr darstellt als die Spur dieser Erfahrungen, ebenso musikalisch wie still, um die Verwerfungen der Wirklichkeit besser erfassen zu können.

Alexandra Baudelot
Kunstkritikerin und Schriftstellerin

A travers ses photos Caroline Halley des Fontaines nous ouvre à un monde où l'évocation de soi et de l'autre est un geste qui réaffirme pleinement la place de l'homme.

Une à une, au fur et mesure que se découvrent les multiples facettes de cet univers, les images nous parlent. Elles nous racontent une histoire qui parcoure les pays d'un bout à l'autre du globe, sans soucis des frontières, sans liens apparents à une culture qui les distinguerait les unes des autres. La profondeur de l'image ne réside pas dans son lieu d'enracinement. Les environnements résonnent, évocateurs des chemins que l'homme a dû parcourir pour s'arrêter un jour, parfois par choix, parfois par asservissement involontaire.

Ces images ont mille visages et pourtant nous pouvons affirmer d'elles qu'elles n'en ont qu'un. Celui d'une humanité traversée par son histoire millénaire, celui ramené à une silhouette, à un regard, à un geste fulgurant que l'œil de la photographe saisi et qui nous raconte le mouvement incessant par lequel l'homme n'a de cesse de se construire. Devant ce visage se déroule un temps qui s'impose dans le silence. « Le temps et le silence » nous dit-elle. Avec ce seul titre en guise d'annonce à une expérience intime, nous sommes invités à parcourir le temps en laissant derrière soi les fantasmes des sociétés modernes attachées à leurs conquêtes, aux technologies, aux désirs générés par une vie de loisirs.

Notre regard fait ici l'expérience de la perte et du glissement vers d'autres territoires. L'artiste ouvre par petites touches les éléments poétiques, spirituels et politiques qui constituent au figuré le monde dans lequel elle déambule, en corps à corps, en prise avec un réel transitoire.

A travers cette implication très forte avec son sujet, elle nous invite à prendre la mesure d'une perte ancestrale, à découvrir les signes vibrants qui demeurent au cœur des sociétés en lutte permanente pour leur devenir. Devenir, c'est à dire aller vers autre chose, vers un ailleurs qui conserverait cette part d'humanité irréductible à chaque être. Un ailleurs situé dans un entre-deux, saisi par l'image, entre le poids du quotidien et un imaginaire versé dans l'intemporalité. Ainsi en est-il des femmes dans les prisons en Inde, des tibétains dans leurs lieux d'exil, des touaregs sur un lieu de mémoire, des hazâras dans leur lieu de refuge ou encore des masaïs à travers leurs rituels.

Dès lors, nous envisageons le chemin qu'il nous reste à parcourir pour ne plus avoir recours au quotidien pour parler de soi à la première personne mais pour le vivre comme une expérience de soi déclinée au pluriel. L'image est donc tout à la fois un lieu de construction et de perte. Elle s'attache à un monde qui ne se lirait pas que par le prisme de ses mises en scène. Le réel apparaît ici en se dessinant peu à peu dans des fragments de brume, dans des halos de lumières qui percent l'obscurité ; élégance de l'esthète qui s'abandonne dans la contemplation éphémère, accompagnement respectueux de son sujet teinté d'une distanciation d'où affleure des mystères que la photographe entend bien préserver. Le temps se décuple à l'infini et les espaces se superposent.

Les photos de Caroline Halley des Fontaines invitent à un univers où c'est la démultiplication de l'expérience saisie dans toute sa fragilité qui impose sa structure narrative. Un monde – une histoire – où l'image n'est que la trace de cette expérience, musicale autant que silencieuse, pour mieux atteindre les failles du réel.

Alexandra Baudelot
Critique d'art et écrivain

Biography

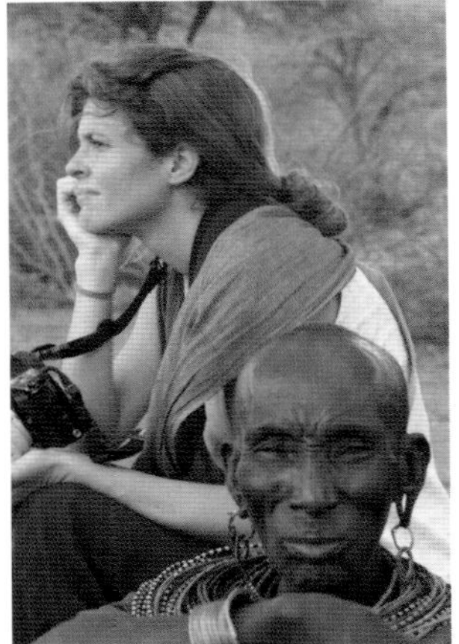

2007–2008
Photographic and Video Work, "Babel – The Boundaries of Knowledge"
Photographic and Video Project on Women and Femininity (Portraits)

1999–2006
Photographic Project, "Time and Silence" on Vanishing Cultures, Memory and Freedom Issues

Shooting in India (Women's Jail, Jaipur), Tibet/Nepal/India (The Tibetan Culture and the Exile Path), Afghanistan (The Hazara from Bamiyan), Cambodia (Memory of Angkor), Kenya (Vanishing Tribes of Samburu), Sri Lanka (Slavery and Tea Plantations), Ethiopia (The Keepers of the Temples of Lalibela), Egypt (Tuaregs' Rememberings)

Sponsors
Fuji Co.; Leica; Dupont Lab; Kodak (Sponsor for Young Talents); Bianimale Foundation, New York City

Partners
Penal Reform International (PRI); Amnesty International; AINA, Paris/Kabul;
Enfants Réfugiés du Monde Organization, Paris/Kigali;
Tibetan Foundation (Switzerland – Spain – USA); Accor Group; Air France...

1998
Design and Realization of a Personal Photographic Project on Freedom Issues
Research for Partners and Sponsors

1995–1998
Human Rights Officer in International Organizations
India – Morocco – Vietnam – Rwanda

1989–1995
DESS Sociology of Development
Master in Law and Human Rights
University La Sorbonne, Paris

Acknowledgments

The great masters for their inspiration.

The Prince of the Elephants for his confidence and faith, Isabelle Menu for her printing talents, Philippe Dian for his encouragement, Jean Michel Cambillou for his long-term collaboration, Klaus Hebben for his tremendous support, Jacques and Martine Debras for their strength and guidance, Alan Kozlowski and Emma for their support, Olivier Ponsoye (and Tiare Group) for their fidelity, Daniela Batteleur and the Douglas Hamilton family for sharing their love, experiences and knowledge about Africa, Jean Francois Camp and his team at Dupon Lab for their magic advice, Mathieu Ricard and Raphaelle Demandre for opening their doors in the Himalayas and sharing their spiritual path, Bob Thurman for telling Buddhist stories, Aina and Manoocher in Kabul for their trust and assistance, Mohamed for telling the secrets of the pyramids, the team of the Bianimale Foundation for their work (Yoyo, Gloria and others), Ursula Vollenweider for her presence, Dominique Leidi for her link in between art and spirituality, Fuji Co. for their film supply, teNeues Publishing team for taking care of this book, Camera Work AG Gallery and its team for their talents and visions...
All those who were supportive all along with the project in their own way: private photo collectors, Alexandra Baudelot, Charlotte Leouzon, Arland Wrigley, Alice Audouin, Mamad, Roberto Giori, Nancy Abraham, Guili Cordara, and, of course, my family.

All the local communities that I met on the path who opened their doors, families and hearts to the foreigner that I am.

Exhibitions

March – April 2008
Solo Exhibition, "Time and Silence," Camera Work Gallery, Berlin

2007
Camera Work Gallery, Berlin
Photo London
Paris Photo

May 2007
Solo Exhibition, "Urban Zen Temple" – Art Installation (Photo/Video), Stephan Weiss Studio (Donna Karan), New York City

November 2006 – January 2007
Exhibition, "Indianscope" – Art Installation (Photo/Video), Maison de la Photographie, Lille (Lille3000 Festival)

September 2006
Solo Exhibition, Stephan Weiss Studio (Donna Karan), New York City

May – June 2006
Solo Exhibition, "The Exile Path" – Extract from "Time and Silence," Tiare Exhibition Space, Paris

January 2006
Solo Exhibition, "Time and Silence," Contemporary Art Gallery Rabouan-Moussion, Paris

May – June 2003
Solo Exhibition, "The Exile Path" – Extract from "Time and Silence," Lugano

January 2003
Los Angeles Photo Fair
Solo Exhibition, On the Path Gallery, Santa Monica – Los Angeles

November 2002 – January 2003
Exhibition, "Regards Rebelles," IRIS Gallery, Paris (Month of the Photography, Paris 2002)

2001
Solo Exhibition, "Freedom with no Wings," European Parliament, Brussels
(First World Wide Congress against Death Penalty)

May 2000
Exhibition, "The Bosniac World," EDF Exhibition Space, Paris

Caroline Halley des Fontaines is respresented by:

Camera Work GmbH
Kantstraße 149
10623 Berlin
Germany
Phone: +49-30-310-077-3
Fax: +49-30-310-077-50
www.camerawork.de

For limited edition prints of all images included in the book, please contact Camera Work Gallery, info@camerawork.de, phone: +49-30-310-077-3

Caroline Halley des Fontaines
13, rue Charlot, 75003 Paris, France
Tel.: 0033-6-0769-6138
e-mail: carolinehalley@wanadoo.fr

www.carolinehalley.com

Photographs by Caroline Halley des Fontaines
Poem "Time and Silence" by Caroline Halley des Fontaines
Translation by Gudrun Gründken (German)
Essay by Alexandra Baudelot
Translation by Zoratti studio editoriale:
Anne Slater (English), Birgit Irgang (German)
Editorial coordination by Arndt Jasper, teNeues Verlag
Production by Nele Jansen, teNeues Verlag
Layout by Eva-Maria Reuters, ereuters@t-online.de
Color separation by ORT, Krefeld

Published by teNeues Publishing Group

teNeues Verlag GmbH + Co. KG
Am Selder 37, 47906 Kempen, Germany
Tel.: 0049-(0)2152-916-0, Fax: 0049-(0)2152-916-111
e-mail: books@teneues.de

Press department: Andrea Rehn
Tel.: 0049-(0)2152-916-202
e-mail: arehn@teneues.de

teNeues Publishing Company
16 West 22nd Street, New York, N.Y. 10010, USA
Tel.: 001-212-627-9090, Fax: 001-212-627-9511

teNeues Publishing UK Ltd.
P.O. Box 402, West Byfleet, KT14 7ZF, Great Britain
Tel.: 0044-1932-4035-09, Fax: 0044-1932-4035-14

teNeues France S.A.R.L.
93, rue Bannier, 45000 Orléans, France
Tel.: 0033-2-3854-1071, Fax: 0033-2-3862-5340

www.teneues.com

ISBN: 978-3-8327-9242-8

Printed in Italy

Bibliographic information published by Die Deutsche Bibliothek. Die Deutsche Bibliothek lists this publication in the Deutsche Nationalbibliografie; detailed bibliographic data is available in the Internet at http://dnb.ddb.de.

teNeues Publishing Group
Kempen
Düsseldorf
Hamburg
London
Madrid
Milan
Munich
New York
Paris

teNeues